Business NOT as Usual

Ian I. Mitroff

In collaboration with
Susan A. Mohrman and Geoffrey Little

Business NOT as Usual

Rethinking Our
Individual, Corporate,
and Industrial Strategies
for Global Competition

 Jossey-Bass Publishers

San Francisco • London • 1987

BUSINESS NOT AS USUAL
Rethinking Our Individual, Corporate, and Industrial Strategies for Global Competition
   by Ian I. Mitroff

Copyright © 1987 by: Jossey-Bass Inc., Publishers
                     433 California Street
                     San Francisco, California 94104
                              &
                     Jossey-Bass Limited
                     28 Banner Street
                     London EC1Y 8QE

Library of Congress Cataloging-in-Publication Data

Mitroff, Ian I.
   Business NOT as usual.

   (The Jossey-Bass management series)
   Bibliography: p. 181
   Includes index.
   1. Industrial management—United States. 2. Organi-
zational change—United States. 3. Industrial organi-
zation—United States. 4. Competition, International.
I. Mohrman, Susan Albers. II. Little, Geoffrey,
1956–   . III. Title. IV. Series.
HD70.U5M52   1987   338.9   86-46333
ISBN 1-55542-030-3 (alk. paper)

Manufactured in the United States of America

The paper in this book meets the guidelines for
permanence and durability of the Committee on
Production Guidelines for Book Longevity of the
Council on Library Resources.

JACKET DESIGN BY WILLI BAUM

FIRST EDITION

Code 8721

The Jossey-Bass Management Series

Consulting Editors
Organizations and Management

Warren Bennis
University of Southern California

Richard O. Mason
Southern Methodist University

Ian I. Mitroff
University of Southern California

Preface

There comes a time in the life of every nation when piece-meal, stop-gap solutions to its basic problems no longer suffice. Then, if it is to survive, it must turn its energies away from treating symptoms and deal honestly with its true problems. Our nation has reached such a critical point. The overvalued dollar, skyrocketing internal deficits, and a balance of payments that is out of control are all serious symptoms of deeper problems. The deeper problems—to which we must now attend—result from America's failure to produce quality products that can compete in world markets. At the root of that failure is the inability to realize that the rules of doing business have changed because the world has changed fundamentally and that the rules are never going back to what they were when America first became great.

For all practical purposes, all business today is global. Those individual businesses, firms, industries, and whole societies that clearly understand the new rules of doing business in a world economy will prosper; those that do not will perish.

The conditions on which America's early success was built have changed. Institutions that served us well in the past are now in need of fundamental redesign. In many of the nations we compete against, public and private institutions have already undergone radical redesign. Clearly, many of our foreign competitors understand that the new rules for competing in the world economy flow from different kinds of social institutions. In our own country, dramatic upheavals in virtually every one of our basic industries, professions, and organizations are unmistakable signs that we are beyond superficial quick-fix remedies or piecemeal tinkering. Now deep changes are needed in the structures of our institutions and in the mental attitudes of the people who work in them.

More than ever, top executives and managers need to have a broad understanding of the many and varied forces that have shaped today's global economy. This book is intended to help them understand and deal with those forces, which affect the internal workings of their firms as well as the external milieu in which their firms must function. The book is also intended for a more general audience of readers who wish to understand why the old ideas—on which we have based our practices for so long—no longer work in the current interdependent global economy. Students and scholars in the social sciences who are interested in the global economy will also find this book of value.

This book is based on the work we have done over the past fifteen years through various consulting, workshop, research, and teaching assignments in organizations. Our work has mainly consisted of helping major public and private organizations redesign their strategic missions, organizational structures, and practices so that they can survive in environments that are increasingly more complex and turbulent.

In the past five years in particular, top executives and managers with whom we have worked have expressed their clear understanding that it is "no longer business as usual." Global competition has forced them to recognize that if they and their organizations are to survive, let alone prosper, they will have to learn to manage and to think very differently.

The replacement of old assumptions with new ones is one of the main concerns of this book. To make this conceptual shift as accessible as possible to the reader, at the beginning of each chapter we have provided a list of contrasting propositions or assumptions. These lists allow quick comparison of the ideas that have been appropriate in the past with the new ones that are appropriate for the revolution we are going through now. This shift in assumptions can be glimpsed through the following examples:

Assumptions underlying past business and management practices	*Assumptions underlying business and management practices in today's global economy*
1. Enormous slack in the U.S. economic and social system, for instance, in the form of cheap energy, labor, raw materials, and huge domestic markets have rendered the U.S. safe from foreign competition and intrusion; room for sloppy, inefficient management.	1. Little or no slack available to any one player in the world market; if anything, the slack we once enjoyed has now passed to other countries; the U.S. no longer possesses the advantages of cheap labor and its huge domestic markets are no longer safe from foreign intrusion.
2. The domination of world markets by one or two top players for relatively long periods of time.	2. The end of long-term domination of world markets by any one player, although those that understand the "new rules" of the world economy can gain significant short-term advantage.
3. Government participation in industrial policy is disallowed; government is the *enemy;* government assistance is socialistic and leads to centralized state planning and control.	3. Government participation is absolutely essential to coordination of a complex policy for competing against nations that have the active assistance of their governments; government is an *ally;* government assistance does not signify socialism, but is part of the "new capitalism."
4. If it ain't broke, don't fix it.	4. Since the system is now so complex, a break in any

Assumptions underlying past business and management practices

Assumptions underlying business and management practices in today's global economy

one part affects everything else; one averts catastrophe by anticipating breaks and fixing them before they actually happen.

5. Workers and managers alike do not need to understand the whole business and to participate in its planning and running.

5. Everyone connected with an organization needs to have a broad understanding of the whole system if the company is to produce quality goods that can compete in world markets.

6. Global marketing is unnecessary.

6. Global marketing is absolutely critical; all markets are now worldwide.

7. Bigger is better; growth is the single most important indicator of the health of an organization.

7. Less is more; running lean and mean is the new order; downsizing is the new critical advantage.

8. Bureaucracy is the best form of organization; standardization and mass production are the keys to success.

8. Bureaucracy is the worst organizational form for competition in a global economy; ability to adapt to shifting markets and consumer tastes is essential, along with high-quality products and services; hence, new forms of organization are evolving at a rapid pace.

Overview of the Contents

This book is divided into three parts. The first part, entitled "The End of 'Business as Usual,' " discusses how the world went from being organized largely in our favor to being organized more to our disadvantage. In Part One, we look at the large domestic markets, isolated from foreign competition, that were the foundation of America's early success, and also at today's world markets that are so strongly interconnected that virtually none of them are safe from foreign encroachment. We examine why, in this new world, businesses and societies need to understand how to think, organize, and manage with a global orientation in order to prosper.

Part Two is entitled "New Ways of Thinking, Organizing, and Managing in a Competitive World." This part discusses the new rules and strategies for doing business in a global economy from the standpoint of a single individual, an organization, an industry, and, finally, from that of our entire society. The analysis we provide of the ways each of these levels affects the others is a distinctive feature of this book. We emphasize the premise that all change that is fundamental affects all of society, not just one or two aspects of it.

The third part of the book, "New Thinking for Complex Times," is concerned with giving the reader broad comprehension of why changes are needed in international business practices. The basic argument is that in complex as opposed to simple systems, unrestricted growth will prove disastrous. Thus in simple systems, "bigger is better"; but in complex systems, at some point, bigness turns against itself and leads to system collapse. Growth management as well as control of positive and negative features are fundamentally different in simple as opposed to complex systems. Since complex systems interact strongly they are less able to prevent their negative aspects from influencing their positive features. The third part of the book focuses on these fundamental differences and on why is it necessary to think, organize, and manage in new ways in today's environment.

Major Themes

Because the theme of global thinking is so central to the major thesis of the book, we need to make clear the special sense in which we use it. *Business NOT as Usual* is not intended as a guide for doing business in all quarters of the globe. It does not, for example, discuss the countries of the Third World that are just emerging as competitive entities in the world market. This is not because such countries are unimportant but, rather, because the new rules are most clearly seen in countries whose global policies are well defined and functioning, notably the Asian countries.

Likewise, it must not be interpreted that because we devote considerable attention to Japan and stress the lessons that can be learned from the Japanese, we are unqualified supporters of their policies. (In reality, our observations are hedged with qualifications. There are some indications, for example, that Japan's recent economic successes may have been achieved, in part, through intensive ethnic cohesion that has racist overtones. If this is the case, it may prove to be an Achilles' heel in Japan's otherwise admirable global strategy.) We dwell so heavily on Japan because that country is our most important industrial competitor. Nearly half of our trade deficit for the current year is expected to be incurred with Japan.

There are other, deeper reasons as well for concentrating on the Japanese. They are the developers of the world's most successful industrial policy to date—a national strategy for targeting and supporting industries for competition in the world market. We do not advocate that the United States form an industrial policy (IP) such as the Japanese have. Indeed, we have always had an IP of one kind or another. The question is whether the fragmented IP we have now is appropriate for today's highly competitive environment. Thus, we discuss Japanese policies *not* with unqualified endorsement but in the spirit of raising fundamental questions about ourselves.

In considering the evolution of organizations—or of entire societies—there are four primary stages that can be identified. They are survivability, viability, growth, and development. At the survivability stage, the main concern is with obtaining the minimum requirements necessary for existence. At the viability level, enough goods are produced and enough income generated to ensure day-to-day existence. At the growth stage, the entity—organization or society—is more than self-sustaining; it supports a larger number of people than it could in its initial stages and may be able to achieve a position of dominance within its markets. Further, its productivity is increasing measurably each year. Development is very different from the previous stages. Development is characterized by a shift from focusing on the goal of quantitative increases in performance indicators to improvements in the quality of life for people who belong to the organization or the society.

The United States, and virtually all of the Western industrialized nations, has been obsessed with quantified growth. World conditions are now forcing a shift from quantitative concerns to qualitative ones. It is a difficult change; after so many years of measuring success quantitatively, growth has come to be confused with development. Russell Ackoff has put the distinction admirably well: "Cemeteries grow each year, but they don't develop."

It is unlikely that the United States can remain an undisputed leader in the growth of the world's markets. But it can become a leader in development. The difficulty is that "success" in the past has pertained to growth. Illuminating the shift to development and America's ability to achieve it is our primary purpose in writing this book. We believe that if we in the United States continue to be obsessed with growth, not only will we not develop, we will in all likelihood be thrust back from the conditions of growth to those of survival.

In sum, *Business NOT as Usual* is intended as a guide to the patterns of thinking that are required to forge new strategies for succeeding in today's global environment.

Acknowledgments

A number of people read the manuscript, or parts of it, and offered valuable criticisms. Although we assume full responsibility for the final version, we offer our thanks for their sage advice to Vincent P. Barabba, Raoul Carvajal, Richard Chase, William Davidson, James Hodgson, Frank Hotchkiss, Irving Margol, Mark Pastin, Jane Pisano, Mark Pisano, Robert Reich, Lester Thurow, Theodore Williams, and Harold Willens.

Susan A. Mohrman and Geoffrey Little helped with or were responsible for portions of the manuscript. Chapter Four, in particular, was largely due to Mohrman's efforts; in addition, she critiqued and helped shape the entire manuscript. Geoffrey Little participated in the formation of the basic idea of the book. He and I are collaborating on a script for a series of television programs based on the ideas in this book.

Lastly, I wish to thank my family for their support, understanding, and help throughout the writing of this book.

February 1987   Ian I. Mitroff
                                                         Los Angeles, California

Contents

The Author

Ian I. Mitroff is Harold Quinton Distinguished Professor of Business Policy in the Graduate School of Business at the University of Southern California. He received the B.S. degree in engineering physics (1961), the M.S. degree in structural engineering (1963), and the Ph.D. degree in engineering psychology (1967), with a strong minor in the philosophy of social science, all from the University of California at Berkeley.

He is a member of the American Association for the Advancement of Science, the American Psychological Association, the American Sociological Association, the Institute of Management Science, the Philosophy of Science Association, and the American Academy of Management.

He has published over one hundred articles and books in professional journals and popular magazines. He wrote one of the first books on crisis management and is the codirector of the Center for Crisis Management at the University of Southern California. Above all, he is interested in the relationship of theory to managerial practice and practice to theory. He is especially concerned with the development of theories of social science that are of direct interest and relevance to practitioners. He no longer believes that the gap between theory and practice is relevant to the kind of world in which we live.

Principal Collaborators

Susan A. Mohrman is a research scientist at the Center for Effective Organizations, Graduate School of Business Administration, University of Southern California. She received her A.B. degree (1967) from Stanford University in psychology and her Ph.D. degree (1978) from Northwestern University in organizational behavior.

Her research has focused on organizational design, innovative organizational systems, and quality-of-worklife projects. She is currently conducting comparative studies of cooperation between labor and management. In addition, she is working closely with several high-technology firms to develop a sociotechnical design model for that industry.

Geoffrey Little is currently director of National Program Underwriting for WQED, the Public Broadcasting Service station in Pittsburgh, Pennsylvania. He holds a B.A. degree (1980) from the University of Pennsylvania and the Annenberg School of Communications, with a major in communications.

Little's main work has been in developing, producing, and writing national programs for the Public Broadcasting Service, among them "The Chemical People," with Nancy Reagan; "Breathing Easy"; and the forthcoming "Conserving America." With Ian I. Mitroff, Little is developing a television series on managing change.

Business NOT as Usual

It must be considered that there is nothing more difficult to carry out, nor more doubtful of success, nor more dangerous to handle, than to initiate a new order of things. For the reformer has enemies in all those who profit by the old order, and only lukewarm defenders in all those who would profit by the new order, this lukewarmness arising partly from fear of their adversaries, who have the laws in their favor; and partly from the incredulity of mankind, who do not truly believe in anything new until they have had actual experience of it.

Niccolò Machiavelli
The Prince, 1537

1

Unmistakable Signals: Something Dramatically Different Is Happening Out There

"The U.S. once saw itself as an economic island, so large and strong and independent that it could all but ignore the rest of the world. That view has long been obsolete . . . [recent] events . . . provided fresh and painful evidence of how closely American interests are tied to decisions made in other countries" (Greenwald and others, 1985, p. 52).

Executive Summary

Old Organizing Ideas	New Organizing Ideas
1. Things really don't change; they just recycle.	1. The change occurring today is so substantial that it cannot be met with traditional tools.
2. All problems can be broken down into component pieces and solved independently of one another.	2. No significant problem can be solved independently of any other significant problem.
3. Society is evolving toward ever-increasing regulation; the possibility of deregulation is unthinkable.	3. There is no such thing as complete protection.

1

Old Organizing Ideas	*New Organizing Ideas*
4. "If it's not broke, don't fix it."	4. Perpetual in-place fixing is the new order of things. Breaks must be sensed before they're fully apparent and, hence, become catastrophic.

The Glacier Effect

This is how a top executive at one of the United States's major entertainment firms sees the problem that American businesses and the economy as a whole face:

> I think most businesses today are the prisoners of what I call "the glacier effect." If you look at a glacier at any moment in time, it appears to be sitting still. You know in your head that it's constantly creeping along but it's doing it so slowly that at any point in time you can't see its movement. Thus, it's always possible to say that the glacier and all that it represents really doesn't affect me. I think this is how the vast majority of U.S. businesses have reacted to all the changes taking place around them. They've either denied their existence altogether or they've pretended that they were occurring so slowly that they didn't have to take them into account, or that they had plenty of time to adjust to change. For instance, to take one example, at any point in time the U.S. auto companies could deny that radical changes were occurring in the car-buying tastes of the American public or in the quality of the cars being produced by the Japanese. Believing that this was so, they not only denied that the glacier was moving at all, but stronger still, they denied its very existence. One day they awoke to find that the glacier was not only bearing down on them in their own backyard

but that it had actually rolled over and flattened them during the night when they were asleep feeling very fat, comfortable, and cozy.

This executive is not alone in his sentiments. In the past five years in particular, we've been privileged to talk to and to work with some of this country's top executives. We've noticed a substantial change in their attitudes. They are more aware of the changes occurring around them and they are more inclined to do something about them.

High-level executives are keenly aware of and more concerned with broad economic and social issues that affect them and their organizations. It is especially significant that this is true across the widest array of industries, from banking, manufacturing, and oil to food, entertainment, and even public service industries such as law enforcement. Visionary executives are more likely to sense issues before they are fully apparent to everyone and to ask themselves What can we do to prepare ourselves to deal with important issues before it's too late—before they have run over us?

Astute executives list a large and varied set of conditions in the environment external to their corporations that now affect them. In one large company with which we have worked, a top-management task force identified a group of issues (Table 1) that show the wide variety of changes occurring in the United States and in the world. These are the issues with which top executives, in particular, must concern themselves.

**Table 1. Changing Conditions That Are Forcing Top Executives
to Consider Far-Reaching Changes in Their Businesses.**

Competitive Conditions

- Increased low competition from every corner of the globe
- Lack of market domination by one organization, industry, or country
- Competition with government-subsidized foreign competitors

Work Force

- Availability of laborers, domestic and certainly international, who are willing to work for less

(continued on next page)

Table 1. Changing Conditions That Are Forcing Top Executives
to Consider Far-Reaching Changes in Their Businesses, Cont'd.

Work Force, Cont'd.

- Anticipated shortage of skilled labor
- Waning union power
- Illegal immigration
- The "new" employee: more questioning, higher expectations, less loyalty, less willingness to move
- Flexible work force (contract, part-time), core versus others
- Changing demographics of work force: women, dual-career families, atypical life-styles
- Greater emphasis on individual rights and workers' changing attitudes toward the importance of work in their lives

Economy, Financial Environment

- Strong U.S. dollar
- Fluctuating currencies of foreign nations
- Change from a manufacturing economy to a service/information economy
- Huge federal deficits, limiting funds that corporations can borrow for expansion
- High interest rates
- High benefit costs
- Increasing costs of health care
- High cost of labor in the United States
- Ongoing ramifications of oil crisis, uncertainty about energy, lack of long-range planning
- Unknown effects of new tax legislation
- Questions regarding stability of social security system
- Large percentage of money allocated for defense
- Affordability of social programs (who will pay?)
- Increasing cost of higher education

Corporate Financial Organization

- Greater utilization of outside contract services for key components of firms' products
- Mergers, takeovers, and acquisitions at an unprecedented rate
- Customer partnerships and joint ventures
- Fear of hostile takeovers that drain time and money
- Offshore manufacturing

Market

- Fewer, bigger customers who can demand and control more from their suppliers
- Bigness of corporations a disadvantage in a time of rapid niching by small companies
- Shorter product life for all goods and services

Table 1. Changing Conditions That Are Forcing Top Executives
to Consider Far-Reaching Changes in Their Businesses, Cont'd.

Regulatory Environment

- More government regulation
- Deregulation of industries

Technology

- Rapid technological change
- Increased need to train and retrain employees at all levels of the organization
- Large investments required for new technologies (robotics, for example)
- Increased potential for technology failures leading to catastrophes
- Shift of nuclear energy from an asset to a liability
- Ability to manufacture new products in space
- Improved communications and mobility: events can quickly become known worldwide
- Need to manage more information more efficiently
- Obsolescence of middle and upper managers with respect to computer skills

Production Emphases

- Improvement of quality (build it right the first time)
- Reduction of inventory costs (just-in-time manufacturing)
- Robotics

Natural Resources

- Uncertainty over future energy sources
- Possibility of water shortages

Societal Trends

- Aging population requiring health benefits and social programs to meet their needs
- Litigious society, employee rights (everyone sues anyone)
- Consumer movements
- Increasing use of drugs on and off the job
- Special-interest groups (homosexuals, women)
- Shortage of technical-field professors in colleges

Worldwide Politics

- Increased threat of kidnapping and terrorism
- Decaying infrastructure of cities
- Political instability in the Third World
- Increasing chance of initiation of nuclear war by a Third World country

What's especially distressing to top executives is that all the issues described in Table 1 are bearing down on them simultaneously. One issue would represent a formidable challenge, but together they represent sheer havoc and chaos. Worse still, these issues no longer act independently; they interact and reinforce one another in strange and unpredictable ways. Businesses deal well one at a time with issues that can be separated from one another. They know far less how to think about, let alone deal effectively with, such interconnected issues. This is precisely the difference in today's world. There are not only more glaciers with which to deal but they come unpredictably from more directions at once. And as if this weren't trouble enough, the glacier effect has shifted into high gear. The glaciers and the changes they represent no longer creep along; they overtake us in rapid succession.

No single book could possibly ever deal with all of the issues in Table 1. Hence, that surely cannot be our goal in this book. What we can do, however, is show how and why the nature of today's environment has changed so dramatically that it is now virtually impossible for an important issue to act in isolation. Any issue or event anywhere and anytime can now be linked in strange unexpected ways with another event or issue. Most important, in Chapter Three we present a set of guidelines for thinking through any issues in Table 1 and, especially, for coping with interconnected issues. As we shall see, this ability to think through such linkages is critical in today's environment.

The World of Banking as a Prime Example of Strange Interconnectedness

Few industries highlight the changes this society is experiencing as clearly as does the banking industry. Consider the fate that recently befell savings-and-loan associations (S&L's) in Ohio. (A few months later, a nearly identical series of events occurred in Maryland.)

On March 4, 1984, ESM Government Inc., a Florida securities dealer, collapsed because its risky trading investments went bad. The following week, Home State Savings Bank, which one commentator labeled as "a distinctly *minor-league* [emphasis ours] Cincinnati savings-and-loan" (Morris, 1985, p. 3), also closed its doors. More than one-third of Home's loan portfolio was invested in ESM securities. One week later, the value of Great Britain's enormous North Sea oil inventories dropped 8 percent in five days as an "indirect" result of what happened to the S&L's in Ohio.

What kind of world has it become wherein the fate of S&L's in Ohio is tied to that of an obscure securities firm in Florida and, further still, wherein the value of British oil stocks is in turn linked to the events in both Ohio and Florida? What could possibly connect these three events in such different regions of the globe? Examination of the sequence of events may help us more fully appreciate the differences in today's world.

The road to understanding begins with recognition of what has happened to more industries and professions than at any other point in our nation's history: deregulation, one of the key issues listed in Table 1. Banks were once tightly regulated by federal laws with respect to the amount and kind of interest they could offer on investor accounts. Deregulation changed this in one fell swoop. Almost overnight, banks, S&L's, and mortgage, security, and investment houses found themselves in fierce competition, encroaching on each other's traditional businesses. As a consequence, not only were they forced to become more competitive, but many had to learn how to compete for the first time.

The strength of this new competition is illustrated in an article from the April 15, 1985, edition of the *Los Angeles Times*. California Safeway stores, already one of the largest cashiers of personal checks in the state, announced that 217 of its stores would be equipped to accept bank machine cards issued by all California banks. The new electronic system would expand the possible users to 12 million by adding banks and S&L's that were not previously part of the network. These include California's five largest banks: Bank of America, Crocker, First Interstate, Security Pacific, and Wells Fargo. In the style that has come to be typical of such encroachments, Frank Nowakowski of City National Bank, which operates the 200-

bank Instant Teller Network, proclaimed, "It's going to make a lot of financial institutions sit up and take notice" (Broder, 1985, p. 3).

As if the pace of change weren't fast enough, a mere ten days later, Sears unveiled a new credit card, Discover, which offered features not provided by other general-purpose cards such as Visa and MasterCard. With Discover, users can purchase goods and services from retailers other than Sears (for example, airlines, hotels, and stores). In addition, users can obtain emergency cash and cash checks, and they are also automatically protected in case the card is lost or stolen. Further, Sears will offer cardholders an exclusive family savings account that will feature a uniquely tiered interest accruement structure. Finally, Sears is negotiating to make its new card compatible with existing nationwide automated tellers so that Discover users can withdraw their money anytime anywhere. With Discover, we have in effect realized the single, all-purpose financial institution. Banks as we have traditionally known them are virtually obsolete.

Regulation had not only limited the levels of interest institutions could offer customers, but more important, it had limited the kinds of investment packages and services they could offer. As a result of deregulation, traditional savings institutions, in particular, were forced to make riskier investments so that they could offer the much higher rates of return consumers had come to expect from these institutions. But this meant that somewhere along the line one of those risky investments was bound to fail for legitimate or illegitimate financial reasons. Such failures are inevitable, given that success is never a sure thing. Thus, this part of the chain of events is normal. It is the other part of the chain, the link among Florida, Ohio, and Great Britain, that is not traditional and that makes today's business climate so different.

What happened to an admittedly "minor league" S&L in Ohio had distinctly "major league" repercussions. It sent major shocks throughout the national and international financial markets. This occurred because the world's financial markets are now extremely skittish over the United States's financial condition (high federal deficits, inflation, fate of long-term interest rates, huge debts of Third World countries to U.S. banks and the catastrophe that would occur if these countries failed to make good on their loans, general health and long-term growth prospects of U.S. and world economies, and so on). Anything that comes along and taps these underlying fears is bound to set off sharp and severe reactions. In this case, the reaction was a sharp drop in the value of the U.S. dollar against other world currencies. It occurred because the world feared that the deficit-ridden U.S. financial system was strained to the hilt and that Ohio was just a signal of the worst that could happen.

In response to these worries, there occurred a series of events that tied everything together. Between March 18 and March 20, 1985, the U.S. dollar fell against the British pound in one of the largest drops ever recorded in the history of floating exchange rates (Greenwald and others, 1985). But because British oil assets are measured and traded directly in U.S. dollars, those holding British oil assets took a severe beating. Hence, the chain of events was now complete. What initially began as a regional crisis in a minor-league Ohio S&L ended in an international incident. Little matter that like so many of the recent crises, this one seemed to subside quickly and was brought under control by sweeping Ohio S&L's under federal bank charters to protect their holdings. The fundamental point remains: We are more interdependent at every level of society than at any point in world history. *Everything everywhere now truly has the potential to affect everything else.*

Implicitly, and in most cases explicitly, the top executives with whom we have consulted recognize the multitude of issues that affect all businesses directly and indirectly. They recognize less strongly that the old methods by which they have run their businesses are no longer working, although there is growing recognition that the game can no longer be played by the old rules. It is no longer "business as usual." They are beginning to realize that they cannot deal with isolated issues one at a time and, further, that they cannot wait until the entire glacier is upon them before they take action. By then, it will be too late. They must learn to anticipate issues and to deal with as many of them as they can simultaneously.

It has long been an axiom of business that "if it's not broke, don't fix it." If we had to sum up the import of this chapter in a few words it would be this: The world today requires not only more fixing, but new kinds of fixing as well. It requires anticipation of breaks in the system and initiation of the repairs before the breaks are fully apparent. *Perpetual in-place fixing is the new order of things.*

Finally, one last but encouraging word. Even if organizations don't yet know how to deal with important issues that interact simultaneously, there is a hopeful sign. Many executives are no longer looking for simple answers to complex problems. We find them increasingly willing to entertain far-reaching, open-ended, critical give-and-take discussions on key issues that do not terminate in simple, quick-fix solutions. More than anything, this may make it possible for executives to utilize the more sophisticated methods that exist for dealing with complex problems (see Mitroff and Kilmann, 1984).

2

The Slack Is Gone:
How We Lost
Our Competitive Edge

"Immediately after the Second World War the United States enjoyed a crushing economic advantage because its productive machinery was more modern than anyone else's (and had not been bombed). But by the early 1970s the forces that would eventually destroy South Chicago were being set in motion around the world. As investment capital became more mobile, companies were freer to shop for locations with lower wages and better "business climates," whether in Tennessee or Taiwan. The oil-price increases engineered by OPEC [Organization of Petroleum Exporting Countries] in 1973, and the resulting inflation, reduced the standard of living for most Americans —but not for workers in the heavy industries, whose unions had negotiated the cost-of-living adjustments known as COLAs. This was a temporary advantage for [the workers] and a long-term disaster for their industries. During the late 1970s, when chronic inflation eroded the dollar's value in international trade, American goods became artificially attractive to foreign buyers—and American manufacturers were lulled into an artificial sense of security about their ability to compete. They were not prepared

Note: The analysis offered in this chapter is based primarily on the following works (but is not solely confined to them): Ackoff, 1981; Kilmann, 1984; Mitroff and Kilmann, 1984; Piore and Sabel, 1984; Reich, 1983; and Scott and Lodge, 1985.

to adapt when circumstances changed in the early 1980s and an overvalued dollar drove their foreign customers away" (Fallows, 1985, p. 56).

Japan's leading kaisha [companies] are often its leading exporters. The patterns of competition they exhibit in Japan are often the same used in Western markets. Being in Japan and successfully competing with the kaisha is probably the best assurance a Western company has that it will be prepared to compete with them in Western markets. In doing so the executives of the Western company will be very aware of the product offerings of the kaisha, how these are marketed, the characteristic price levels, and the anticipated technological developments.

Almost all executives, Western and Japanese, would claim growth to be one of their principal goals. However, the goals of Japanese and Western management can be quite different. In a recent study reported by the Japanese government, the corporate objectives of about 500 major U.S. and Japanese companies were compared. . . . the responding executives of U.S. companies ranked return on investment as their principal corporate objective. Share price increase was ranked second and market share third. . . .

The U.S. ranking is in sharp contrast with that of the responding executives of the Japanese companies. Market share was ranked first, return on investment second, and the refreshment of the product portfolio third. Share price increase was last among Japanese corporate objectives. . . .

Judging from the realities of competition, the elevation by U.S. management of the return on investment goal over the goals of market share and refreshment of the product portfolio would seem to be illogical [Abegglen and Stalk, 1985, pp. 176–177].

Executive Summary

Old Organizing Assumptions	*New Organizing Assumptions*
1. The U.S. corporate bureaucracies created between 1870 and 1930 represent a *permanent* solution to the problem of how to organize a society for economic production.	1. Corporate bureaucracies represent *only one* solution at best.
2. U.S. domestic markets are so large that manufacturers can safely ignore the rest of the world. U.S. markets will never be saturated for traditional consumer products and they will always be homogeneous.	2. No markets anywhere can be safely ignored. One has to be prepared to compete everywhere. U.S. markets have become saturated for traditional consumer goods, and tastes everywhere have become differentiated into niches.
3. The United States has an enormous edge in terms of cheap labor, energy, technology, and vast resources which will never be used up.	3. We've lost (perhaps forever) our competitive advantage in terms of labor, energy, technology, and resources. The only advantage left is creative imagination if it can be harnessed properly.
4. The raw materials of the underdeveloped countries can serve indefinitely as strategic reserves to the U.S. economy.	4. The underdeveloped countries have learned to harness their reserves to their own strategic advantage through the use of the latest technology.
5. The dominant position of the United States in the world economy allows it to run up long-term feder-	5. No country is immune to radical ups and downs in the value of its currency.

Old Organizing Assumptions	*New Organizing Assumptions*
al deficits without devaluing the dollar.	
6. Significant social movements do not have profound effects on the social structure and the economy of the United States.	6. The women's movement and the Vietnam War altered significantly how both men and women viewed work.
7. Every rule of business that has made for success in the past will make for continued success in the future.	7. Every rule that made for success in the past has to be rethought because its unreflective application can lead to failure.

Before one can correct a situation, one must understand how and why one got into it. Otherwise, the solutions may merely recreate the problem on a new level.

In this chapter, we investigate why the world changed from a place where critical issues could be dealt with separately one at a time to a place where all issues interact at blinding speed and, hence, must be dealt with collectively. As we shall see, we went from a world, and, in particular, a nation, into which enormous slack had been built in the form of cheap labor, energy, vast resources, and technological and organizational superiority, to a world in which fewer advantages are available to any single player in the international game of business and economics. In the past, our incredible resources could buffer, if not isolate, us from the rest of the world. We have exhausted our buffer. The slack is gone.

Until recently the symptoms of trouble were too slight and infrequent to make us realize that we had not solved the problems of economic organization forever. We failed to appreciate that the huge U.S. corporations that were created between roughly 1870 and 1930 constituted only *one* solution at best to the problems of organizing a society for the effective creation and distribution of wealth. Many solutions are possible. Further, we forgot that the modern corporation evolved only half-consciously through a highly nonlinear process of experimentation fraught with trial and error. It certainly did not emerge full blown as the result of an overall, grand design. It is essential to realize that the modern U.S. corporation was organized primarily to create large standardized (that is, stable) markets to which it could then supply the goods it produced in large amounts. Creation of such markets was necessary to justify and protect the enormous capital investments required to produce large batches of standardized products. To put it somewhat differently, once the United States made the half-conscious "decision" to abandon the innumerable small, craft businesses, which were the hallmark of the nineteenth century, and go the way of producing and consuming standardized products, both organizations capable of mass production and stable markets capable of mass consumption had to be created. Neither arises naturally. Both are social inventions.

To appreciate that none of these points is merely theoretical or academic, consider what's changed. Thirty years ago it took some forty years between the introduction, or birth, of a product (say a refrigerator) and its saturation, or death, in the entire market, partly because of the long time between adoption of a new product by the opinion leaders and the diffusion of such products to the masses and partly because of the high cost of new products. Hence, for whatever reason, products and markets were extremely stable and, thus, predictable.

Today, with mass marketing, relatively low costs, and mass communication, the time between introduction of products and their saturation is shrinking to virtually zero. This creates problems for manufacturers. How does a manufacturer decide what to produce, for whom, for how long, and at what cost? How does one know that the market (i.e., demand) for a particular product will not shift before that product is made? Part of the answer, as we shall see, lies with the Japanese, who have learned to construct a different industrial structure which shifts quickly in response to changing consumer demands.

Complicating this further is the fact that U.S. and world markets are even less homogeneous than they were some twenty to thirty years ago. Ironically, in spite of the great cultural diversity of the immigrants, one of the reasons why mass markets

have succeeded for so long in the United States is that compared with others, such as Europeans, Americans have more standardized tastes. In large part, this was due to the desire of immigrants to assimilate into the "melting pot." Further, because the
U.S. market was itself so large, U.S. manufacturers could virtually ignore the rest of the world and concentrate almost exclusively on internal markets. These and other factors contributed to the feeling that not only were we invincible but we were
ordained to occupy a privileged and protected place in history.
The short of it is that we took the constancy of our economic
environment for granted. We could in effect plan for what people wanted and would consume without planning in the traditional sense, that is, centralized state planning. We had created
a system and a society for which centralized planning in the
overt sense was unnecessary because planning was *covertly* built
into the design of our principal economic institution, the modern corporation.

   None of this is meant to imply that the control over its
environment achieved by the modern corporation was perfect.
Indeed, the Great Depression of the 1930s vividly demonstrated that the modern corporation was at best a partial solution to the economic problems of the United States. By organizing as it did, the modern corporation had achieved partial
control over its external markets; however, because the market
as a whole was ultimately dependent upon the prosperity of the
entire national economy, complete control was beyond the
power of corporations. For this and other reasons, government
increasingly came to be viewed as having to play a critical role
in managing (stabilizing) the economy. By not insisting on bal-
ancing the federal budget every year and by stimulating the
economy through programs that benefited various segments of
the population, the federal government acted to lessen the effects of severe economic ups and downs. In this way, it sought
to ensure a greater constancy of economic behavior to the supposed benefit of all. For instance, the U.S. government financed
90 percent of the federal highway system and thereby not only
directly stimulated the automobile and construction industries
but in effect showed them preference over other industries.

Certainly this was a national industrial policy of the highest order. To say therefore that we don't need industrial policies today when the environment is much more turbulent is to ignore the fact that we've always had such policies. (We shall examine more thoroughly the arguments for and against national industrial policies in Chapter Six.)

Although they in no way approached complete harmony, the government and the large corporations did move steadily toward working in accord. Not to be left out, big labor also worked to ensure the constancy of its side of the coin, that is, employment and wages. But by the same token, because the large corporations now had a big stake in maintaining the mass markets they had worked so hard to create, they also had a big stake in maintaining the constancy of labor's purchasing power even if they couldn't admit this publicly. The more the society as a whole subscribed to a mass consumption as well as a mass production economy, the more sensitive it became to the ups and downs of the purchasing power of consumers. This meant that it was in the direct interests of both labor and management to reach wage-setting agreements that would stabilize income for labor and costs of production for management. The granddaddy of all these agreements may well have been the 1948 accords between the United Auto Workers (UAW) and General Motors (GM), which tied wage increases to increases in labor productivity and to changes in the consumer price index.

As helpful as these institutional mechanisms were in forestalling unpredictable and rapid increases in labor costs and hence in the eventual cost of goods, they also had some powerful unforeseen consequences that foreshadowed the even greater and more traumatic consequences that operate in today's world. Although the various wage-setting formulas helped to stabilize the economy to the greater benefit of both labor and management, they had an unintended effect—curtailment of the previously unhampered workings of a so-called free market—which in turn limited the ability of wages to signal to corporate and governmental decision makers where resources needed to be shifted from one industry to another to redirect the economy. Wages in all industries had increasingly become linked so that an attempt to recruit workers from one region to circumvent wage-setting formulas in another region failed as a long-term strategy. The only way to get around such formulas was through what slack still remained in the economy, for example, the large pool of nonunionized, semiskilled labor reserves in the South. The unintended effect, however, was that the economy became increasingly dependent on such slack resources for the versatility it required to maneuver around constraints. The problem today is that virtually all the slack has been expended. As a result, we as a society have nothing left to give us a critical edge in competing in world markets. Because of the enormous gains made by labor, U.S. workers have become priced out of world competition in many industries.

This does not put the blame entirely on the U.S. labor movement. Rather, it points out that in dealing with a large and complex system, it is vital that one be extremely sensitive to forces that on the surface appear to be beneficial to all (wage-setting agreements) but may actually contain some potent, long-term, negative consequences. One wishes in retrospect that we could have designed better wage-setting mechanisms, which would have improved the lot of workers everywhere but would not have curtailed the ability of wages to signal the need for detailed and specific changes in critical parts of the economy as well as the economy as a whole. If anything, the whole wage structure for both labor and management has grown increasingly out of line with the world economy. For example, the wages of top executives in the United States exceed those in Japan dramatically.

Both labor and management bought in equally to the solutions of that era. Thus, in stressing that the future of the automobile industry is tied to negotiations with the UAW, *Business Week* noted:

> Accustomed to prosperity without competition, both sides let efficiency and quality decline. Executives at GM and Ford admit that management is to blame for at least 80% of the industry's problems, including botched product designs, poor capacity utilization, and bloated staffs. . . .

During the 1970s, productivity gains were eaten up by soaring wages and benefits that pushed the labor content of an average new car to $2300. Many analysts expect productivity among U.S. auto companies to improve by an annual average of only about 5% over the next three years. This compares with 10% average yearly productivity gains in Japan, where labor rates are increasing at only 5% annually. One result: Japanese cars now claim 17% of the U.S. market, despite voluntary restraints. . . . Once the quotas are dropped, some analysts say that Japan could snare some 35% of the U.S. market by 1987 ["Showdown in Detroit . . . ," 1984, pp. 104-105].

Both intentionally and unintentionally, the U.S. economy came to depend on slack in countless ways. For instance, because of its dominant position in the world economy, the United States played an almost colonial-like role with regard to the underdeveloped nations before and after World War II. The raw materials of the underdeveloped countries were available almost on demand to U.S. markets at the best prevailing world prices. These raw materials served as strategic reserves to the U.S. economy, much as the unskilled labor reserves of the South had earlier. Further, its dominant position also allowed the United States to run up long-term federal deficits without having to devalue its currency. All of these actions allowed the United States to quell potential destabilizers of its economy. Their cumulative effect was to addict the U.S. economy to artificial devices. When these props collapsed, as they must do eventually, the economy was sent reeling in a manner similar to an addict whose daily fix has been abruptly withdrawn. The economy had lost its ability to cope without props.

All of the forces acting to reduce the slack on which the U.S. economy had relied for so long came to a final head in the midsixties and early seventies. The world was racked by a number of crises that were to irreversibly change the nature of international economy. First, the United States experienced a number of movements that not only effected permanent changes in its social structure but also changes in its economy. For instance, the women's movement and the protests against the war in Vietnam changed not only the social expectations of women and other minorities in the United States but also the attitudes of the general population which underlay the wage-setting formulas between labor and management of previous generations. As a result, wages were no longer constrained by the written and unwritten social contracts of the past. In short, all workers, but especially women and minorities, wanted more and were tired of waiting for it.

Second, the United States was finally forced to abandon the gold standard. It could no longer run up the huge deficits that it had, for instance, in paying for the Vietnam War, without devaluing the dollar relative to foreign currencies. But this meant that both the value of the U.S. dollar and the price of U.S. goods were increasingly subject to distant economic forces which were neither connected directly to the performance of the U.S. economy nor under its control. At the same time, the world economy was becoming increasingly dependent on what happened everywhere. Certainly the fate of European economies was no less tied to what happened in the United States. As *Business Week* put it, "Europe's [economic] fate still depends critically on what happens across the Atlantic. The vaunted decoupling of Europe from the U.S. is still a long way off" ("The World Can't Shrug Off a U.S. Showdown for Long," 1984, p. 51). These global international forces, coupled with the saturation of internal U.S. markets for traditional consumer goods and the breakup of the demand for standardized goods, had a devastating effect on the mass production economy that characterized the United States.

If this were not enough, the two oil shocks in the 1970s wreaked havoc throughout the Western economies. Because everything was tied in to the availability of cheap energy, the sharp, dramatic increases in oil prices sent cataclysmic waves of inflation throughout the West. The effects were increases in the prices of virtually all goods and pressure for wages to rise in accordance. Finally, the whole world was thrown into an economic downturn because of the rippling effects of unprecedented high U.S. interest rates.

The worst, at least from the standpoint of the United States, was not over yet. The final blow came on two fronts: the Third World countries and Japan. By the end of the 1960s both the Third World countries and Japan began to change the rules of the international economic game. According to conventional economic theory, the Third World countries should export to the developed countries what they had to trade, namely cheap raw materials, which would then be transformed into finished products and sold back to those same countries at a higher price, thus ensuring a balance of payments in favor of the United States. Some Third World countries learned to play a different economic game. They used their cheap labor to a cost advantage in favor of finished goods that they now produced. (The irony is that this is the same strategy that the United States had developed early in its history and had now forgotten as a mature economic power.) Further, they trained their labor to do high-quality, technical work. Countries such as Japan and Korea created new financial and market institutions to favor their goods on the world markets. For example, they rewrote their tax codes to favor certain industries and even encouraged their banks to offer cheap loans to the favored industries.

Countries such as Japan and Korea refused to remain second-rate economic powers, which they would have been forced to do if they had followed the rules of the game formulated by David Ricardo and his followers some 200 years earlier. According to Ricardo, a nation should produce and hence export products to the rest of the world based on the resources with which nature has endowed it. But if this were the case, it meant accepting as natural and inevitable those constraints that nature chose to dictate to a country. If a nation was endowed with second-rate natural resources, it was thus doomed by natural economic laws to be a second-rate economic power. Much to the dismay of the United States, Japan and the Third World countries learned, as we shall see in the next chapter, to challenge and to overthrow these "natural constraints." At the same time, Japan learned how to structure industry based on a different mixture of principles. They learned how to combine the advantages of both mass production and specialized craft industries in a new form. What the Japanese did was to create an industrial structure based from top to bottom on flexibility. It was a craft industry in the sense that it was geared to producing high-quality, specialized goods. It was a mass production industry in that it was geared to producing these goods in great numbers. It was based on flexibility in that it was able to shift very quickly when the market for a particular good appeared near saturation or when it was no longer profitable to produce a certain good.

In response to these competitive threats, U.S. companies tried various strategies, none of which really worked effectively for long. For one, companies diversified into various types of businesses. They merged with and acquired one another at unprecedented rates. They engaged in paper entrepreneurship at record levels; that is, they engaged in paper shuffling (manipulating accounts), creating profits on paper, but not where it counted, in actual reinvested capital for future productive capacity. These tactics didn't work because the threats to U.S. businesses now arose from threats to the economy as a whole. Thus, addition of businesses to businesses that were already threatened only increased the magnitude of the overall threat. For another, U.S. businesses tried to produce world products. This no longer worked, because international markets were now organized not around homogeneous tastes but along increasingly differentiated tastes. Hence, to sell well, one had to sell refined. Again, the United States needed flexibility to produce products that were adaptive to the special markets around the world.

While these trends were taking place, other events were also occurring that hampered even further the ability of American business to compete effectively in the new world economy. By 1984, *Business Week* could report that "Figures compiled by the Labor Dept. show that pension plans governed by ERISA (Employee Retirement Income Security Act) regulations control some $1 trillion in capital, concentrated predominantly in corporate stocks and bonds. On average, institutions account for 80% to 90% of all daily trades" ("Will Money Managers Wreck the Economy? . . . ," 1984, p. 88). The significance of this report lies in the fact that the people who manage and control ERISA have an extremely short-term perspective on the

U.S. economy. Their concern is with immediate profits (this quarter). This puts enormous pressures on companies to manage the present and to discount almost entirely the future. To do this means sacrificing long-term ventures, innovative products that cannot by definition always show an immediate profit, or businesses that are marginally profitable but show indications of becoming profitable in the future. It also means foregoing needed capital investments and the development of innovative techniques of production and management necessary to renew an organization's capacity to respond to the changing economic environment.

The top business executives with whom we and others have dealt are not necessarily happy with these conditions. In the same *Business Week* article in which the report on ERISA appeared, a number of executives reported their intense dissatisfaction with what's been happening. Greg A. Smith, executive vice-president of Prudential-Bache Securities, observed that "the typical investment cycle was three to five years in the 1960s. Now . . . it's more a casino operation" ("Will Money Managers Wreck the Economy? . . . ," 1984, p. 92). And Edward D. Zinbarg, senior marketing director of Prudential Equity, noted, "The short-term emphasis ultimately hurts the whole economy, [but] I don't know what you can do about it" ("Will Money Managers Wreck the Economy? . . . ," 1984, p. 92). Finally, Leon G. Cooperman, partner of Goldman, Sachs, one of the largest investment firms in the United States, observed, "I don't think any company can afford a long-term investment today unless its managers own 51% of it" ("Will Money Managers Wreck the Economy? . . . ," 1984, p. 93). These views encourage U.S. companies to play it extremely safe at a time when they cannot afford to do so.

Again and again on every front, the United States has struggled to learn three lessons, lessons that it still struggles to learn today. One, it has used up its material and strategic reserves of slack. The only slack remaining is the boundless energy, creativity, and self-confidence of its people. Two, the age of unrefined mass production and mass consumption is over. The age of highly refined and specialized niche markets and, at the same time, paradoxically, mass niche markets has arrived. Three, *every rule of the game that has made for unqualified success in times of stability and plenty now has the potential to produce the exact opposite effect in times of severe worldwide competition.*

None of this should really be surprising. For if history teaches us anything, it is that when faced with crises, the majority of people and institutions repeat what got them into the crisis in the first place. They blindly repeat and even intensify the actions that worked well under one very special set of conditions in the hope that they have found a permanent magic solution

Among the recurring patterns that cause problems for our businesses are the following:

1. Getting sucked up into the general malaise that is so prevalent in our culture, that is, the belief that there is "one best way" to approach all problems or that for each problem there is only "one best answer" to it, and therefore constructing a rigid hierarchy that reinforces that there is only "one best way."

2. Sticking to and enforcing rigid cost and management formulas, narrow programs, tired products, and inflexible production quotas long after they have ceased to serve their original intended functions.

3. Attending only to the immediate, short-term problems and issues, focusing on details, seeing only the parts, and thus ignoring the long term, not attempting to see beyond the horizon, failing to grasp the whole by not placing all problems within the total context, losing sight of the overall objectives of the entire organization and the entire economy.

4. Judging the performance of something so huge and so complex as an entire organization in terms of single and simplistic standards such as the "bottom line," and thus, at best, treating as second priority or, at worst, ignoring the multitude of all the other competing standards on which the modern organization has become increasingly dependent (for example, health and general welfare of its customers,

employees, and the surrounding community and environment in which it does business and upon which it depends in order to do business).

5. In sum, failing to be aware of the implicit and unstated assumptions that have guided our industrial development in the past and failing to change them if they are no longer appropriate for the current environment (see Mason and Mitroff, 1981).

In this chapter, we have deliberately reported the bad news because, unfortunately, it is real and there is no use in ignoring it. Fortunately, there is also good news. If our important industries have literally had to reach the point of death, at least many have gotten the message that they cannot do "business as usual" and are changing. It is these organizations to which we turn in the remainder of this book and spell out what needs to be done. In the next chapter, in particular, we discuss the new kind of thinking required for survival today.

3

Thinking Beyond
Conventional Strategies:
Consider the Extraordinary

"There aren't a thousand people in this nation who are good integrators of knowledge. . . . We have those who know all about highflying exotic X's and nothing about something over here, and what you have in crisis decision making is not specialized decision making. It is the integration at the highest levels of lots of information and requires people who can with confidence, span . . . areas. . . . But if you generally haven't trained people with that capability—and we're a long ways away from training them at the level [of the] White House—you're in for serious trouble" (Richard Beal, quoted in Smith, 1984, p. 908).

"At best, the current system of education prepares young people for preexisting jobs in high-volume, standardized production. Some students are sorted into professional ranks and trained in the manipulation of abstract symbols. Others are prepared for lower-level routine tasks in production or sales. Few students are taught how to work collaboratively to solve novel real-world problems—the essence of flexible-system production" (Reich, 1983, p. 215).

Executive Summary

Old Organizing Assumptions	*New Organizing Assumptions*
1. All important problems have a single correct solution or are solvable in principle.	1. It is of vital importance to differentiate whether a problem is to be solved, resolved, or dissolved.
2. Constraints are to be respected.	2. Constraints are to be treated with discourtesy.
3. Solving a problem demands that one focus or define it as narrowly as possible.	3. Resolving or dissolving a problem demands that one define it as globally as possible.
4. Assumptions are irrelevant; end performance is all that counts.	4. Assumptions are the fundamental "glue" of all social life.
5. To be successful, one must work within accepted, conventional notions.	5. To be successful in today's world, one must identify basic assumptions and "flip them on their heads."

We want to begin outlining the kinds of new skills that are needed for survival in today's world. In this chapter, in particular, we discuss the kind of critical thinking required to deal with the extreme interconnectedness that is a fundamental feature of all complex issues.

From the Ordinary to the Outrageous

Sixteen years ago, a sociologist by the name of Murray Davis published a fascinating article (Davis, 1971) entitled, appropriately enough, "That's Interesting." It shows as powerfully as any single source we know why ordinary thinking is no longer adequate in dealing with the issues described in Chapters One and Two. Davis set out to answer the following question: Why do people consider social scientists like Karl Marx and Sigmund

Freud "great," whether or not they agree with these scientists? Davis's answer was not that they produced theories which were somehow truer and better than those produced by the average mortal, for there are no perfectly true theories in science. Theories are merely approximations which break down at some point and hence fail what they purport to explain. Reality is too complex to be captured by a single theory, no matter how powerful it is.

Davis's contention was more subtle and hence more interesting. He proposed that the great social scientists were great precisely because they produced theories that were "interesting." Aha! But what makes a theory interesting? According to Davis, an interesting theory does three things: First, it raises to the surface an assumption in which a significant body of people believes almost without question. Second, it very strongly challenges that assumption. And third, it develops a strong, completely opposite, counterassumption.

A simple example is the view of the human mind before and after Freud. Before Freud, the assumption was that the complete contents of the mind are available for inspection by consciousness. After Freud, the counterassumption was that significant parts of the mind are not accessible to consciousness and, indeed, are repressed from consciousness by unconsciousness. Hence, Freud produced a theory that is interesting because he showed how the mind conspires against itself to prevent it from being known both to itself and to others.

Davis points out, however, that "interestingness" is a very tricky business. If a speech or paper affirms a group's belief, the likely response is "that's obvious!" and, hence, "that's not interesting!" On the other hand, if one, and certainly if *all*, of a group's most sacred assumptions is strongly challenged, as in Chapter Two, when we challenge what many Americans would still like to believe about the U.S. economy, then the likely response is "that's absurd!" or "that's outrageous!" and, hence, "that's not interesting either."

Davis didn't plot his insight on a graph, but if he had, the result would have looked something like Figure 1. The "O" stands for the "that's obvious" region, the "I" for the "that's

Figure 1. Degree to Which an Assumption Is Challenged.

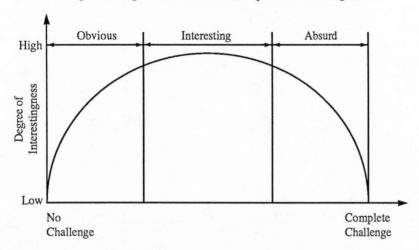

interesting" region, and the "A" for the "that's absurd or out-rageous" region. Note that the two extreme points, extreme obviousness and extreme absurdity or maximum challenge to one's beliefs, are perceived by most people as uninteresting. We think that this simple figure helps us determine the exact heart of what's different about today's world.

Look at Figure 2. At the top, we've placed some critical events roughly where at one point in time they might be located along the continuum between obviousness and absurdity. Although everyone may not agree with our placement of particular events, we intended that Figure 2 indicate, on the basis of our experience, easy versus difficult matters with which most people deal. For example, Mitroff and Kilmann (1984) have given a series of talks on corporate tragedies, including the Tylenol poisonings and the Bhopal disaster. Audience reaction indicated that for most people these events are clearly in the extreme parts of the A region. They represent a complete breakdown of normality. They represent a world gone completely beserk through forces most people can neither comprehend nor deal with either intellectually or emotionally. Many people prefer not to recognize such phenomena, let alone realize that such incidents occur close to home.

Figure 2. Degree to Which One's World Is Challenged.

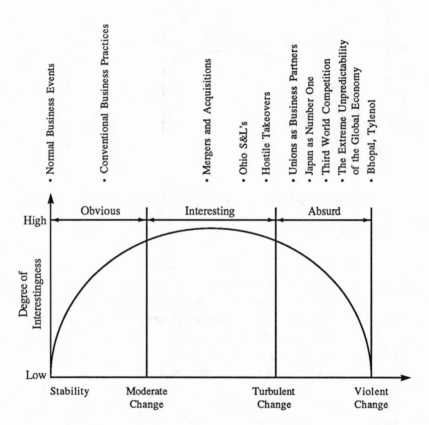

From our collective experience, it's also clear that most people, at best, have been trained and are willing to move only marginally into the I region. One could argue, and we would agree, that the most innovative companies foster an environment that encourages people to move much further into the I region than they would on their own. It's well known from social science research that groups can either retard or enhance the risk taking or innovativeness of their individual members. It's also our experience that the ability to move farther into the I and A regions characterizes top executives and their teams.

We thus have a fundamental gap between the phenomena

with which the vast majority of individuals and organizations are faced and those with which they are mentally and emotionally prepared to deal. There appears to be no slowing down whatsoever in both the rate and the number of phenomena intruding from the A region. If individuals and organizations are going to cope with these phenomena, they have no choice but to learn the kind of thinking that is best suited to coping with the extremes of the I and A regions. People must learn to cope with realities which challenge their fundamental assumptions. If extreme challenges to the existing order evolve from these regions, then extreme creativity and entrepreneurship evolve from them as well. Thus, we must learn to deal with phenomena in the I and A regions—to cope with extreme disturbances and also to grasp the most creative opportunities. The hallmark of creativity is the ability to move deeply into the A region; to tolerate the extreme anxiety that is associated with the ideas found there which, by definition, go completely against the grain of conventional wisdom; to recognize the faint outlines of an idea that will revolutionize human affairs; and, finally, to move that idea back into the I region so that it will be in a form that is understandable and acceptable to the vast majority who on their own would never tread into the A region.

The following six broad principles are helpful in allowing one to practice "mental judo," that is, to use events in the A region to one's advantage:

1. Seek the obvious, but do everything in your power to challenge and even to ridicule it.
2. Question and challenge *all* constraints. The most limiting constraints are usually imposed not by the problem itself but rather by the mind set of the problem solver.
3. Question and challenge as many assumptions about the problem situation as possible. Remember that what seems self-evident is not always evident to others.
4. Question the scope or definition of a problem. Frequently what's omitted from the statement of a problem is as critical as what's included.
5. Question whether a problem is to be "solved," "resolved,"

or "dissolved." Most people do not appreciate the nuances
that exist between these variations of the verb "to solve."
Each represents a critically different approach.

6. Question logic. Being logical and being right are not always
    the same thing. The more logical a proposed solution to a
    complex problem sounds, the more it deserves thorough
    and unrelenting challenge.

Because so many of these principles refer to the same
thing, we're going to discuss them together.

Undermining the Obvious by Challenging All Constraints

Perhaps no other event in recent times has shown how
vital it is for businesses to challenge the obvious by questioning
all constraints than the deregulation of banks. Prior to deregulation, traditional banks assumed that other institutions would
always be prevented from encroaching on their turf. Thus,
banks took a particular social contract at one point in time as
an inviolable natural constraint. They couldn't have been more
wrong. They were in fact almost dead wrong.

What happened is now well known. For some time prior
to deregulation, Sears Roebuck, the nation's largest merchan-
diser and retailer, knew that it already had in place the
world's largest, computerized, *credit* network. It began to dawn
on Sears that if this credit network could be converted into a
generalized *financial* network, then literally overnight Sears
could become one of the world's largest and most versatile financial institutions. Because it already owned an insurance company (Allstate), and because many of its internal operations and
customer services were already computerized, permitting the
easy and rapid transmission of important information, Sears fig-
ured that by adding other critical financial functions, it could
become a generalized financial service institution for the large
and growing middle-income segment of the population. This
made good sense because it made good business. The large
banks had long since ceased to consider the middle-income segment as a source of new business, because they did not view this

segment as buyers of expanded financial services, such as estate planning and retirement investments. Thus, the banks failed to take such institutions as Sears as a serious source of competition, and they also failed to anticipate the new markets and the new services that would be required and to serve them. Although it was no simple matter to repeal old laws and institute new ones, the federal banking laws were eventually amended. The result, as we all know, is the fiercest competition in almost any industry for consumer dollars.

The principle should be crystal clear: *There is not a single constraint under which any business now operates that should be taken as inviolable for all time.* Indeed, one should routinely list all the constraints under which one currently operates and continually think how impending events could undermine, or at best render irrelevant, each of them. For instance, consider the case of Keffel and Esser. Keffel and Esser was once one of the world's largest makers of slide rules, the small mechanical devices used by engineers and scientists to perform complex calculations before the advent of the small, portable hand-calculator (HC) and the personal computer (PC). Keffel and Esser had assumed that the calculations would always be performed best with slide rules and that therefore engineers and scientists were strongly attached to the product. In a matter of a few years, the HC and the PC completely replaced the slide rule, and as a result, Keffel and Esser was completely excluded from the market. The company had, in effect, been constrained by its own assumptions from entering the HC and PC markets.

The rule is thus to challenge as many constraints as possible. The world, and in particular one's competition, is under no obligation to respect what one takes as a dire constraint. In fact, what one hopes for most is that competitors will be completely hemmed in by the traditional constraints of their business. For this reason, there are two questions a business must ask: *What do we and our competitors take as completely binding constraints? How can both sets of constraints be overcome?* No other questions are more important. These questions must be asked whether or not they have immediate answers, indeed, precisely because they most often will not have immediate answers. The company (or society) that is able to answer these questions—in essence, to find a way around the constraints—is the one that will break away from the pack and have a chance of survival in today's environment.

For example, consider how the Japanese, by flipping a seemingly impossible constraint on its head, were able to turn what seemed to be a decisive disadvantage into an advantage: "Contrary to the conventional wisdom in the West, and in Japan, that Japan is handicapped by its lack of natural resources, the Japanese steel industry actually benefited by not having large domestic supplies of coal and ore. The Japanese companies were forced to search the world for the lowest-cost sources of supply. By contrast, the U.S. and German steel industries have self-inflicted handicaps [that is, constraints] by virtue of their heavy investment in high-cost domestic sources of supply and inland plant locations. As the Japanese have shown in a modern world of free trade, a shortage of resources [that is, a seeming limitation or constraint] does not necessarily mean that a country's population must remain impoverished" (Abegglen and Stalk, 1985, p. 75).

Consider another example. The Japanese have challenged traditional constraints in the design, layout, and utilization of machines and, by doing so, have shown how to obtain significantly greater productivity:

> In Toyota's past, and as it still is in most Western factories today, each machine was manned by at least one worker. The worker figuratively "waits" on the machine: bringing it its material; loading it; starting, watching, and stopping it; unloading it and being responsible for keeping the machine operating or stopping it if it begins to fail. If the worker is skilled (and lucky), management is rewarded with high machine output and utilization.
>
> *The objective of multimachine manning is not high machine utilization but high worker utilization* [italics ours]. The machines are arranged in a "U" pattern. . . . The machines are connected by

roller conveyers to simplify material handling.
Each of the workers is trained to operate several
different machines. The training includes performing changeovers and providing simple maintenance.
Each worker walks in a circular pattern completing
tasks that include loading, starting, and unloading.
The machines are rigged to stop automatically, and
if a machine stops before the worker returns to it,
it waits. The primary objective is to keep the worker busy. Of course, by varying the cycle times of
the machines and the number of machines each
worker operates, machine and worker utilization
can each be maximized [Abegglen and Stalk, 1985,
p. 99].

In short, the above-described design challenged the following
constraints: There has to be one worker for each machine; machines always have to be used in order to justify them; workers
have to be fixed, not mobile; and machines can be arrayed only
in a linear fashion.

If one wants to think creatively, one must learn to love
and to tolerate the questions that challenge, especially those
questions that have no easy, immediate answers. Nothing kills
creativity faster than those old conversation stoppers: "that's
impossible; it's not feasible; it's never been done before because
it can't be done; that's not the way we do it." Entrepreneurs
and the very best executives make it a fundamental point never
to be dissuaded by such stoppers.

Ackoff (1981) gives an amusing but important instructive
example of how thought is often constrained by the all-too-
human desire not to appear ridiculous to one's fellow human
beings. The case concerns an organization that made very small
items of very high value. As a result, the items were easily con-
cealed in a person's clothing and, therefore, were stolen at a rate
greater than the organization could tolerate. At a brainstorming
session, conventional proposals, including highly sensitive metal
detectors and weighing scales, were rejected as infeasible. The
scales, for example, were rejected because the items were too

tiny to be detected by weight. After some time, one participant finally made a highly unconventional proposal: Because the valuables were removed in the clothing, employees should work in the nude, dressing and undressing on the company's premises. Everyone promptly dismissed this proposal with derision.

Fortunately for this company, a subgroup later took the original "outrageous" idea and converted it into one that was plausible. *Working* in the nude was not essential; *inspection* in the nude was. Further, because the items were destroyed by contact with water, the subgroup suggested that workers be required to shower before going home. The ethics of this proposed solution (and we have serious reservations about it) and the possibility that the real problem is something else, such as poor management/worker relations, are also important. Nonetheless, the main point remains: One cannot attain creativity unless one is prepared to court the absurd, to visit the ridiculous, and to raise dumb questions. Indeed, *the raising of at least one dumb question a day is central to the entrepreneur's credo if not to his or her very modus operandi.* Excellent organizations are those which have a greater understanding, appreciation, and tolerance of this behavior in their company cultures. They have a history of sponsoring, supporting, and protecting oddballs and their off-the-wall ideas.

A story in *Fortune* further illustrates the power and the necessity of challenging constraints. Howard Love, chief executive officer of National Steel, couldn't deal with key changes that had to be made in his organization until "he had freed himself from the traditional mindset of his corporate culture" (Magnet, 1985, p. 56). As the steel business worsened and the time came for the rebuilding of his company's coke ovens in Weirton, West Virginia, Love "finally asked himself an unaskable question: Why do we need to make our own coke? That first taboo question led to another, and another. If we don't make our own coke, can our coal operation stand on its own? What about our iron guys—are they competitive? 'Once you start this peel-the-onion type of approach, you can find yourself with some pretty interesting questions,' says Love. A study commissioned from Bain & Co., a management consulting firm, predicted zero growth for the U.S. steel industry, not the 5% to 7% annual growth National had been expecting. And that led to the ultimate unaskable question: Why should National be in the steel business at all?" (Magnet, 1985, p. 56).

By asking questions that challenged long-standing, traditional constraints, Love made the final decision to stay in the steel business but with a twist. Steel would become a "stand-alone" business. It would have to become efficient to support itself. Steel would no longer be *the* business of the company.

Ackoff gives a beautiful example of how critical it is to broaden the definition of a problem before attempting to seek its solution:

A large European city used double-decker buses as its principal means of public transportation. Each bus had a crew of two, a driver who occupied a cab separated from the rest of the bus, and a conductor who had three functions. The conductor signaled the driver when there were passengers who wanted to get off at the next stop, signaled again when to start, and collected fares from those who had boarded. Fares were normally collected when the bus was in motion to make the stops as short as possible. During peak hours this often required the conductor to force his or her way through the crowd on both levels in order to collect fares. Frequently the conductor failed to return to the entrance in time to signal the driver not to stop. [The driver was required to stop unless a signal not to was received.] Therefore, the driver often stopped when there were no passengers to discharge or take on board. Such unnecessary stops bred hostility between drivers and conductors, the drivers being on a meet-the-schedule incentive system, and the conductor being penalized for failure to collect fares if spotted by an unidentified inspector.

The hostility became overt and culminated

in a "war" between the two relevant unions. A
number of efforts to solve the problem by bringing
drivers and conductors together into group discussion failed. Most of these meetings ended in vio-
lence.

An outsider was brought in to help. He
broadened [italics ours] the problem to include
the stops as well as the buses. When this was done
it was discovered that at peak hours there were
more buses operating than there were stops. *This
led to a solution in which conductors were located
at the stops during peak hours, not on the buses*
[italics ours]. Then they could collect fares from
passengers while they were waiting for a bus. Conductors could signal drivers when to start by using
a button located at the rear entrance to the bus,
and passengers could signal the driver when they
wanted to get off by pulling a cord placed around
the sides of the bus. Not only did this reduce delays, but it made fare collection easier. When the
number of buses in operation was less than the
number of stops, at off-peak hours, the conductor
could return to the bus [Ackoff, 1981, p. 179].

The point of this example should be clear. How, after all,
can one cope with a world that is increasingly interconnected
without broadening the definition, and certainly the impact, of
all problems with respect to one another? Indeed, isn't the very
notion of broadening all problems inherent in the concept of a
"global system"? Currently we don't educate people to appreciate this, to ask constantly, and hence naturally, how all problems impact on one another. But then, as we indicated in Chapter One, this lack of questioning is becoming obvious to the top
executives of many organizations.

Before we leave this section, it is important to note that
this simple example contains another very important lesson. It
has to do with the distinctions among "solving," "resolving,"
and "dissolving" a problem. The fundamental reason for broad-

ening a problem is that more often than not it indicates the futility of seeking an exact solution within the original definition of the problem. Thus, in the simple example of Ackoff, it is futile to look for an exact solution to the problem by remaining solely within the definition of the problem, that is, drivers, conductors, buses, and their interrelationships. Once the critical notion of stops is added, one ceases to look for a solution within the limited domain of the initial formulation. One, in effect, "dissolves" the initial problem by taking a broader view. Finally, within the new definition of the problem, one no longer looks for the best solution for all time. Instead, one looks for a solution that is "good enough," a solution that allows a problem to be managed as it changes over time. One "resolves" the problem.

The difference between "solving" and "resolving" is important because it is the difference between handling problems in a simple world and in the complex world of today. In simpler times, problems were supposed to be static. Once a problem was defined, its definition was not supposed to vary. Hence, once a solution was arrived at, it too would not vary over time. *In effect, a problem once solved was solved forever.* The systems age in which we live changed all this. Problems now change as fast as, and in many cases faster than, the solutions can be obtained. Hence, it is now more important to know which are the truly important problems on which to work and which of their definitions are the most fruitful. For example, the Japanese view the problem of worldwide competition as one of producing quality products. Therefore, they employ substantially more engineers than we do in every phase of their businesses, including the shop floor. The United States, on the other hand, views the problem as one of regulation. Therefore, we bring lawsuits and seek government protection. As a result, our society produces and hires more law school graduates than does Japan. What will it take for the United States to redefine the problem as one of producing quality goods that are competitive in world markets?

Companies are finding that the production of quality products demands that they seek a broader definition of their problems. For instance, the change in perspective from reactive to preventive quality assurance is perhaps the easiest mental jump. Even so, it requires a different view of how people should be managed. It also requires changing the whole reward structure of an organization so that people are both enabled and motivated to produce quality products. Ironically, this also requires giving up a fundamental hierarchical principle—task specialization. Quality has to be written into all job descriptions. And further, all employees have to understand clearly how their jobs fit together in the final production of quality products. Finally, quality challenges traditional corporate boundaries. Companies are finding that they have to influence their suppliers to produce quality materials as well.

Thus we arrive at the motto of the systems age: *Far better an approximate ballpark solution to an appropriate definition of the right problem than an exact solution to an inappropriate definition of the wrong problem.* What good does it do to solve the wrong problem precisely? But to solve the right problem requires mental judo. One must be prepared to challenge all constraints, distrust simplicity, question the boundaries of a problem, and, as we see next, challenge as many assumptions as possible.

Challenge All Assumptions

We have been building the case that to cope in a complex environment it is fundamental to raise to the surface and challenge as many important assumptions as possible. This practice is a strong characteristic of creative individuals and organizations.

A colleague of ours, James O'Toole, has recently examined the assumptions upon which one of our major industries, the automobile industry, was based. In a provocative paper, O'Toole (1983) argues that a relatively small set of assumptions, ten in all, can be identified with the initial success of U.S. automobile companies; however, when those same companies failed to adapt to the realities of the times, those very same assumptions were responsible for their subsequent near death or, at the very least, severe economic ill health. Examining the assumptions of General Motors (GM) in particular, O'Toole (1983) states the case succinctly:

> The guiding principles that led to [GM's] early success were crystalized into operating assumptions for all subsequent generations of managers.
>
> All the guiding assumptions were based on the pioneering policies that had made [GM] one of the most successful industrial organizations in the world. By repeating what had made it successful in the past, the company became even more successful. In turn, they reinforced the legitimacy of the operating assumptions. These assumptions then became unchallengeable—and unchallenged. Why challenge an idea with eternal validity? Only a fool would knock success.
>
> *Alas nothing fails like success* [p. 4].

Ten basic assumptions described GM's core belief system as it entered the 1970s (see Table 2). As we all now know, the world changed drastically in the 1970s. The environment caused the assumptions that had served GM so well in the past to become outdated and invalid. Almost overnight, GM's success and its very existence were severely threatened: "Gasoline became expensive; the auto market became internationalized; the rising cost of (and time required for) retooling made it necessary to be a leader rather than a follower in the introduction of new technology; consumer values changed from styling to quality; the size of families shrunk; people could no longer afford to trade their cars in every few years; worker values and attitudes changed; successful government relations required cooperation rather than an adversarial; the few 'kooks' in California who bought Volkswagens and read *Consumer Reports* [became] an important segment of the auto buying public. . . . By 1980 the environment had changed so thoroughly that the brilliant assumptions created by the company's founders to meet the exigencies of the environment of the 1920s were inappropriate in

Table 2. Assumptions and Counterassumptions for General Motors (GM).

Generic Type/Concern		Initial Assumptions		Counterassumptions
1. What is the basic business and who has basic control of the organization?	1.	GM is in the business of making money, not cars. (The accounting and finance people have taken over control of the organization.)	1.	GM is primarily in the business of making quality cars, not money. Any organization that forgets its fundamental purpose for going into business will not achieve one of its fundamental financial objectives. (The engineers and the accounting/finance people should share control.)
2. What must our posture toward innovation be?	2.	Success comes not from technological leadership but from having the resources to quickly adopt innovations successfully introduced by others.	2.	One cannot give up technological leadership in a world that is more competitive than ever. One no longer has the luxury of time in a more complex environment.
3. How does the customer fundamentally view our product?	3.	Cars are primarily status symbols. Styling is therefore more important than quality to buyers, who are, after all, going to trade up every other year.	3.	Quality and styling are equally important in a more competitive market, where even the cheapest car is expensive by past standards and where the competition is able to produce well-crafted and stylish products.
4. How much control do we actually have over our outside environment? How much can we really insulate ourselves from it?	4.	The American car market is isolated from the rest of the world. Foreign competitors will never gain more than 15 percent of the domestic market.	4.	The American car market will never be as isolated from the rest of the world as it once was. Foreign competition is here to stay and it will always be significant.
5. What are the basic resources this organization needs to do business and how available will they be in the future?	5.	Energy will always be cheap and abundant.	5.	Energy will never again be cheap or abundant.

Questions	Assumptions	
6. What are the skills and education required of our personnel to do business?	6. Workers do not have an important impact on productivity or product quality.	6. Even with automation, worker attitudes and skills at all levels are more important than ever.
7. How isolated are we from the shifting concerns of our customers?	7. The consumer movement does not represent the concerns of a significant portion [of] the American public.	7. Given the rising costs of all products and the increasing concern with the environment, there will continue to be some organizations that will represent these concerns. Any organization that ignores these concerns is dangerously deluding itself.
8. What is our attitude toward the government? Whom do we perceive to be our natural enemies? Our allies. Why?	8. The government is the enemy. It must be fought tooth and nail every inch of the way.	8. The government is a significant factor in the environment and as such it must be dealt with whether one likes it or not. It is too easy to blame others for those problems that are due to us.
9. Which type of control is appropriate?	9. Strict, centralized financial controls are the secret to good administration.	9. Compulsive financial controls are the cause and effect of bad administration. There is all the difference in the world between a financial system that *controls* an organization and one that *enables* it to do what it wants to and should do.
10. How closed off is our organization to new ideas? How open, how trusting are we? What's our organizational culture like?	10. Managers should be developed from the inside.	10. The culture of an organization should be continually assessed to ensure that it has not become a closed system that is resistant to new ideas.

Source: Initial Assumptions are taken from O'Toole (1983, p. 4).

the radically altered environment fifty years later" (O'Toole, 1983, p. 5).

O'Toole correctly points out that innovation necessitates continual scanning of the environment for the changes, however minute, that always occur. (See Mason and Mitroff, 1981, for a detailed discussion of how to surface and challenge important assumptions that bear on a business's continued success.) Even more difficult, it requires organizations to act on those changes before it is too late to take advantage of them. It is important to act before one is forced to backtrack from a situation in which one did not want to be.

Table 2 presents a systematic and comprehensive analysis of the ten assumptions that constituted GM's belief system. The table shows the generic concerns or issues represented by each assumption. The table also shows a set of counterassumptions that represent the strongest challenge to the original belief system.

Therefore, the question is not Do we lack either the methods or the tools for challenging critical assumptions? It is Do we have the will to apply the methods and tools?

Some analysts have contended that one of the worst things that could have happened to GM was its announcement of a net income of more than $1 billion for the second quarter of 1983. "[Its] earnings for the year will probably be the best since 1978" (Burck, 1983, p. 100). What's bad about this? It is not that GM is making money once again and showing signs of turning around. Rather, it's that the new success is premature and is still thought by too many within GM to be due to the proven ways of the past:

> The changes GM is attempting are greater in scale and scope than those of the 1970s—indeed greater than anything the company has undertaken since the days of Alfred P. Sloan, Jr. and perhaps un-precedented for any organization of GM's size and complexity. At the same time, *many of GM's 45,500 managers have yet to get the message* [italics ours]. One GM executive glumly mused last

fall that from what he could see, no more than half the company's managers had really grasped the need to change old ways of operating. Overconfidence dies hard, particularly in an organization as conservative as GM. And of course it dies all the harder when sales and profits are moving up [Burck. 1983, p. 100].

What's true of GM is now truer than ever before of all organizations. That the need for change is more drastic and more widespread is clear, however, to some analysts:

Long runs of standardized products brought America unparalleled prosperity. True, that prosperity was interrupted by a great depression and by periodic recessions. But these were interruptions, nothing more. High volume, standardized production always restored prosperity.

America has been unwilling to give up this vision. The present economic decline, after all, superficially resembles earlier ones. Many people cling to the hope that it is also temporary, caused by passing phenomena that have little to do with the underlying organization of American production—"instabilities" in Middle Eastern oil fields. . . . Once these scourges are behind us, so this reasoning goes, America's prosperity will be restored [Reich, 1983, p. 138].

If this is what American business thinks, then perhaps outrageous knowledge is not so outrageous after all. What's truly outrageous is living in the status quo, especially when the cracks in the assumptions upon which the status quo is built become more apparent every day.

There is growing evidence that significant parts of GM, starting with its chairman, Roger Smith, have gotten the message that it cannot operate under many of its old assumptions. We explore this more fully in the next chapter when we discuss

GM's important experiment with the factory of the future, the Saturn project.

In this chapter, we have discussed new ways of thinking and the mental attitudes that must accompany them. The essential lessons can be summarized:

1. Make it a habit to continually list and challenge the constraints under which your current business, industry, or other organization now operates. Also list those of your competition. Make it a point to think how each of these constraints can be undermined. Show what new business opportunities could result from their erosion. Do not assume that any constraint will last forever.
2. Continually ask if you are attempting to solve the wrong problem precisely. Examine how different a problem would look if its definition were expanded or contracted.
3. List at least seven to ten implicit, taken-for-granted assumptions upon which your business was founded and which hopefully made it a success. Ask how these assumptions could be responsible for your business's "failure of success." Ask which assumptions are still valid or invalid.

In the remainder of this book, we show how these ideas are being put to use, both consciously and unconsciously, by innovative individuals and organizations.

4

Building the Organization of the Future Now

"To many observers, GM [General Motors] was the very model of an uncompetitive and nearly comatose American company. Decisions were handed down by managers who seemed afraid to take risks. GM's response to the Japanese challenge of the late 1970s was an unimpressive line of front-wheel-drive cars like the Chevrolet Cavalier and the Oldsmobile Ciera that failed to win many converts from Toyota and Datsun. The problem seemed to be in the sluggish and bureaucratic nature of the vast corporation. Just two years ago, Chrysler Chairman Lee Iacocca was fond of saying of GM: 'Let the elephant sleep. Don't anyone wake the elephant'" (Greenwald, Witteman, and Ungehauer, 1985, p. 57).

Executive Summary

An article in a Harvard Business School research colloquium provides a good summary of old versus new organizing assumptions underlying the design of jobs and organizations (Mills and Lovell, 1985, p. 467).

Old Organizing Assumptions	*New Organizing Assumptions*
1. Jobs are performed best if they are constituted narrowly.	1. Jobs must be broadly defined if America is to produce the high-quality

47

Old Organizing Assumptions	*New Organizing Assumptions*
	goods and products that are necessary to compete in a world economy.
2. Employee skills do not have to be matched to the complexity of the products; thus, specialization of employees is warranted.	2. Employee and management skills/systems have to be closely matched to the complexity and systemic nature of the products necessary for a global economy.
3. Pay should be for specific job content.	3. Pay should be for skills mastered.
4. Evaluation should be by direct supervision.	4. Evaluation should be encouraged by peers.
5. Work must be closely supervised.	5. Self-supervision or peer supervision promotes better-quality products and work relationships.
6. Assignment of overtime or transfer is by the rule book.	6. Teams can be used to cover vacancies.
7. There is no need for career development.	7. Concern for learning and growth must be central.
8. The supervisor must deal primarily with employees as individuals.	8. The supervisor must deal with employees as members of a team.
9. There is no need for employees to be knowledgeable about the business as a whole.	9. Everyone must have an overview of the entire business and feel they are a vital part of it in some fundamental way.

Seeing Beyond the Individual Trees:
Managing the Whole Forest

A recent experience of Mitroff illustrates the problems confronting the outworn structure of many of today's organizations. Not too long ago, he had both the opportunity and the pleasure of working with a research unit of the U.S. Forest Service. On the surface at least, its mission was clear: to provide systematic and detailed research so that the region of the United States in which the unit was located could be managed effectively. Barely beneath the surface, however, were symptoms that indicated all was not well. Not only were there multiple, conflicting notions as to what the unit's "true," overall mission should be, but there was also significant conflict within particular notions.

The unit had been established to serve the needs of a variety of conflicting interests. It was charged with providing the basic research necessary (1) to *preserve* the forest and wildlands; (2) to *manage* the land for proper harvesting, for example, timbering; and (3) to *provide* proper recreational facilities for the thousands of people who annually flocked there. Thus, the unit was torn between conservation and preservation, on the one hand, and land use and economic development, on the other. What kind of research program should it enact under these conditions? The decision to carry out a specific program would support a particular policy of land use.

The real source of the problem lurked deeper beneath the surface. The unit had been organized around specific scientific disciplines that had now become so specialized and fragmented that they made no sense in the particular environment. Thus, the unit was finely subdivided into scientists who were "doctors of bugs and beetles," "doctors of tree bark and pinecone needles," and "doctors of various kinds of small animals and creatures." Despite the multiple conflicting goals and multiple perspectives of Forest Service personnel, the region had to be managed as an integrated, coordinated entity. Although this had always been true, it now was more pressing. The increasing ecological problems affected whole regions, not isolated segments. Therefore, the unit would have to challenge and go beyond the *constraints* of its current organizational structure, that is, the separate scientific specialties would have to join together to build a model of the whole forest.

In many ways, the story of this one unit is the story of organizational America. Whether public or private, large organizations everywhere are struggling to free themselves from the

type of structure that is no longer suited to the kind of environment we have discussed in the first three chapters. We find that
the problem of change is thus generic. In the remainder of this
chapter, we examine several cases that demonstrate some of the
nuances of the changes that will be required of our organizations as they adapt to the global economy.

Redesigning Organizational Structures

Recent experience with a company that designs electronic systems was particularly helpful to us in demonstrating
the tensions inherent in thinking systemically within organizations bounded by traditional assumptions. The company is a
division of a large, well-known, and very successful electronics
corporation. Like so many others, this corporation was staring
at the potential for its own precipitous decline. Previously the
master of a large niche, it had watched foreign competitors in-
vade its markets with less expensive, better-quality products.
And it was becoming painfully aware of its own rigidity because of its difficulty, despite monumental funding, in successfully entering the quick-paced and highly systemic world of
automation.

Meanwhile, this company's small (approximately 500
people), often forgotten, somewhat sleepy, but highly sophisticated systems group was searching for its identity in the emerging new order. Sensing that his group was poorly organized to
assume a role more responsive to the emerging needs of the
corporation, the director of engineering spearheaded an effort
to redesign the organization. What was especially interesting
about this effort was that it was carried out by design teams
composed of key individuals representing the different disciplines, projects, and perspectives in the division. Most of these
representatives were from the various engineering and scientific
disciplines, but the design teams also included representation
from other functional areas, such as production, marketing,
contracts, finance, and human resources. For years these people
had been frustrated in designing, marketing, and selling systems
from within the confines of the nonsystemic corporation. They

had now been asked to set up a systems organization, and they responded to the opportunity with enthusiasm.

The effort began with Mitroff and Mohrman conducting in-depth diagnostic interviews with a cross section of key people in the organization. Summary data were shared with the design teams to stimulate early discussion and provide a foundation. Most notable about the interviews was that virtually everyone had the same perception of the organization and its problems. They described the organization as small, isolated groups, which they referred to as "clumps." The term "clump" was so uppermost in people's minds that a number of individuals remarked with frustration that their organization practiced the "clumponian" theory of management. People in the various clumps communicated with one another with extreme difficulty and, at best, were loyal to their clumps. They had little sense of belonging to the organization, let alone the parent corporation. Individuals with twenty years' tenure admitted to not knowing the names of co-workers in this small organization, even those who inhabited the same halls.

In reality, the company was an organization in name only. It was fractionated along very tight, specialized lines. People were suspicious of, and hostile to, one another, and there was a dearth of communication across complex technological projects and among the various functional groups whose coordinated energies were required for effective functioning in the marketplace. As a consequence, this division was unable to devise, produce, or sell the products that increasingly sophisticated customers demanded. Thus, the design teams were challenged to restructure the organization into one that could devise, produce, and deliver high-quality, complex electronic systems in a timely manner. To promote the values of service and quality in a marketplace in which customer needs were rapidly changing and becoming more complex, they found it necessary to propose changes in almost all aspects of the organization.

The main theme was integration—tearing down the barriers and finding ways to foster teamwork and cooperation. The rigid bureaucracy, with its built-in roadblocks to open, fast communication, couldn't respond in time any longer. Many felt that the company had lost sight of its mission, that customers, marketplace, quality, and productivity had become incidental. Its main purposes had become to protect turf, to build fiefdoms, and to control others but avoid being controlled. This philosophy applied to the internal functioning of the company, as well as to its role within the larger corporation, where it was one of many units, each wanting to coordinate with others only if *it* could call the shots. Indeed, one of the major legitimate complaints about bureaucracies is that they serve themselves instead of their intended clients. Unfortunately, this is true of both private and public organizations.

The team concept would be enhanced by creating a two-tier hierarchy in which project teams reported to a multidiscipline management team rather than one individual reporting to one manager. The separate functional areas would be represented in this higher-level body of appeal, but decisions would

Teamwork became the integrating theme in the redesign. The company was envisioned as a "team of teams." To foster such teamwork, rewards and awards would go to teams, who would then determine whether individuals deserved special rewards. Each project team would be self-contained, in the sense that the necessary skills and functions would be represented; however, in line with the most interesting design feature, individuals would be able to move between levels of teams, between types of teams, and between functional assignments within teams as skills, knowledge, and need permitted. The same individual could be a technical contributor on one team and a leader on another team and, thus, alternate the roles of worker and manager. An individual would be allowed (indeed encouraged) to work on quality assurance on one project and design engineering on another project. Ongoing education and development of breadth as well as depth were to be fostered and rewarded. Where appropriate, "apprenticeships" would be established to enable cross-training on the job. It seemed that people in this organization feared stagnation, that is, becoming locked into a narrow technical specialty, into a role with limited responsibility on a particular project, or into a role that permitted only a partial understanding of the many aspects of the business.

The team concept would be enhanced by creating a two-tier hierarchy in which project teams reported to a multidiscipline management team rather than one individual reporting to one manager. The separate functional areas would be represented in this higher-level body of appeal, but decisions would be made on the basis of multidiscipline considerations. In a sense, all decisions would be made on the basis of systemic considerations.

Thus, the design teams had envisioned a radically different organization—a fluid organization not constrained by rigid, permanent walls. The new organization would comprise teams as well as individuals. *The predominant image was lateral, not vertical.* The key behavioral principles would be to enable rather than constrain, to facilitate rather than control, to coordinate rather than segment, and to share responsibility rather than hoard power.

Unfortunately, however promising and beneficial, this design was not implemented. Independent of the redesign, this division had been merged with a sister division by the corporation and had lost its autonomy. Even before the merger, however, the design teams had encountered considerable negative reaction from authority figures in the organization. Leaders charged with redirecting the business feared loss of control and hence chaos. Functional managers feared the loss of distinct career tracks protected by specialized knowledge bases. The new design flew in the face of the underlying assumptions about how organizations should function. The ideas for change were challenged by defenders of the status quo who attributed problems to the weakness of individuals rather than to the inherent structure of the organization. Members of the design teams, originally chosen because they were considered to be key organizational players, suddenly became branded as "malcontents." And so, the bureaucracy did what it does best—protect its integrity by rejecting new ideas.

Could the new design have worked? Certainly it departed in many ways from tradition. Yet, the cry for new, more *systemic* visions of organization is heard in many quarters; ironically, the parent corporation is one of the leaders advocating change. Thus, customer demand for product compatibility has led such computer manufacturers as Hewlett-Packard and Xerox to reorganize to promote technical interchange and integration in diverse, previously autonomous businesses. AT&T, TRW, and others seek to eliminate expensive redundancy and to use their basic research laboratories to find new approaches to the development and transfer of technology within the organization. Such corporations have decided that they cannot afford to support large sophisticated basic research units, the activities of which may be remote from the business or in conflict with customers.

Perhaps the most public and sobering demonstration of the need for organizations to oversee systems is the 1986 space shuttle disaster. The presidential commission investigating this disaster found that systemic management and organizational problems in the National Aeronautics and Space Administration (NASA) had contributed to weaknesses leading to the technical failure of the shuttle and other accidents (Smith, 1986). The commission recommended establishment of management procedures to improve coordination among the four geographically dispersed space agency centers. One commissioner was quoted as follows: "The centers are little kingdoms unto themselves, and each kingdom has its own king and each kingdom runs its affairs differently. . . . And there are very few ambassadors" (Dolan, 1986, p. 1). The commission further recommended that suppliers and astronauts participate in launch decisions.

Surely the accomplishments of NASA over the past decades must be heralded as among the greatest technical and social achievements in history; yet, even there, bureaucracy became paramount. The elaborate puzzle that must be completed to launch satellites, rockets, and shuttles had become segmented into small, isolated pieces. Higher levels in the bureaucracy had chosen to void the knowledge of lower levels. Managers responsible for pleasing customers had distanced themselves from managers responsible for solving technical problems.

The lesson is straightforward: *to do business in a tightly interconnected world, an organization must take on the properties of the complex environment in which it exists.* Its organizational structure and its products must be matched to its environment. The specific characteristics of the forms of organization needed are not yet fully known, but the broad characteristics—integration, fluidity, and shared responsibility—are obvious. Organizations have become so segmented that they have lost sight of their main purpose. To regain this vision is the *pivotal challenge* before American organizations.

To more fully describe the scope of this challenge, we introduce some concepts that allow us to recap the story of the electronics company and extract some further lessons. We will also draw upon these concepts in later chapters in discussing additional lessons.

Over the years theorists have learned that a few key variables are essential in designing and evaluating an organization. Although individual lists may differ, they share these key variables:

1. Rewards, both symbolic and monetary: What kinds of rewards are available for specific activities?
2. Information: What does the organization consider to be information and how does it acquire and distribute this information?
3. Tasks: How does the organization group its tasks into jobs?
4. People: How does the organization recruit, develop, reward, and keep people?
5. Structure: How does the organization determine the number of levels and division of authority?
6. Organizational culture: What are the organization's basic values and beliefs about itself and its customers? What is its value to society and how do the values of our society compare with those of other societies?

Figure 3 shows the interrelationships of these six key variables. Each variable affects and, in turn, is affected by the other variables. For instance, if the electronics company had truly desired cooperation across divisional lines, then clearly it would have had to change its system to reward interspecialty and intergroup cooperation or, conversely, *dis*reward *non*cooperation. Accordingly, the company would have had to make other structural changes to get this new behavior—for instance, hire people for whom cooperation was a well-established way of life.

Figure 3. The Six Key Variables of Organizational Design.

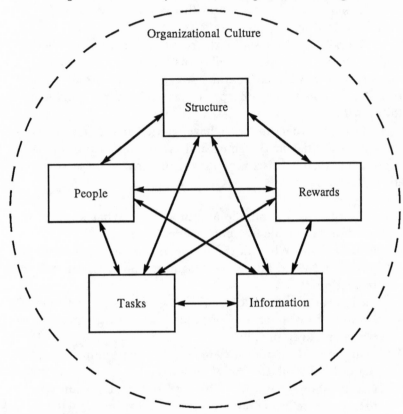

Source: Adapted from J. Galbraith, *Organization Design*, Reading, Mass.: Addison-Wesley, 1977.

Note also in Figure 3 that culture, drawn as a dotted circle, encompasses the first five variables. The culture of an organization pervades all its functions. Because culture is taken for granted, it's simultaneously hidden from view and completely out in the open. For instance, the easiest way to get a handle on culture in a company is to ask the following: If I came to work for Company X tomorrow, what are the *unwritten rules* of the game I'd have to follow to be a success around here? Or, to put it another way, what are the silent do's and don't's? Some typical examples are don't ever bring bad news; don't challenge the boss; always know to whom you're speaking and for whom you work; and be loyal at all costs.

Earlier, we indicated that the design teams realized that a total redesign of the electronics company was necessary. The changes could not be confined to the systems group. The systems group was already dependent on the sales, marketing, finance, accounting, personnel, and manufacturing groups; it would be even more dependent on these groups if it wanted to produce truly integrated products. The *reward* system of the entire company was "out of sync." The company had to shift from rewarding people for being competent in narrow specialties to rewarding people for sharing competency across specialties and, in short, for forming a broader conception of the organization and its products. At the same time, the organization needed to change its *information* structure. Integrated products require manufacturing and marketing data different from those required by more specialized products. In addition, this information, which results from intense cooperation *in the field* among people from sales, engineering, marketing, manufacturing, and finance groups, must be obtained and integrated much faster than before to ensure that the right products are available at the right time for the right customers at the right price.

It became clear that in the long run the organization needed to recruit different kinds of *people*—integrators, or systems thinkers—and, at the same time, retrain its current employees to think systemically across traditional lines of responsibility.

Next, the individual *tasks* needed to be changed and/or combined differently to reflect greater integration.

Finally, the basic *structure* of the organization needed to change drastically. What was required was a structure that contained fewer, but different, levels that were well integrated.

Perhaps the most difficult part of the challenge is to alter the behavior of the millions of hardworking, competent, and conscientious Americans who have become used to, and good at, functioning in large, bureaucratic organizations. To get some sense of what this might take, we next examine the efforts of another company attempting to align its human resource management with the needs of a systems environment.

Does the System Support Itself?

The U.S. aerospace and defense industry is going through its own readjustment period. Such companies have been somewhat buffered from the global economy because their work often is done within the United States for security reasons. In the past, these companies have been relatively buffered from competition as well. Recently, however, the government has cut down on practices that it feels engender waste and inefficiency within government contracting firms, including cost-plus contracts and noncompetitive bidding. Thus the industry is now faced with a competitive environment.

In addition to these changes in the marketplace, there had been a dramatic increase in the sophistication of the products, reflecting the rapid rate of development of technology. Demands for integration skyrocketed; hundreds of thousands of lines of software had to be matched to intricate electronic hardware that must then fit together with components and codes generated from several companies, each of which was authorized to design and manufacture a specific part of the final product.

Recent work with firms in this industry has enabled us to take a close look at the human and organizational sides of the problem. One firm, in particular, decided to examine its reward systems to determine if they fit the needs of the business. The symptoms in this company were similar to those in other large companies. As in the electronics firm we described earlier, there were barriers between parts of the organization. Engineers were accused of "throwing" the finished design over the wall to production. Cost overruns and nonproducible designs led to accusations between two groups with divergent views of the business. These symptoms are well known in many technology-based companies. More fundamentally, however, individuals seemed distanced from the business. Results of a diagnostic survey indicated that although more than 85 percent of the people in the company felt that they were personally doing an outstanding job, a much smaller percentage reported that the projects on which they worked were performing well. Thus, there was a disconnection—individuals could feel good personally about contributions to projects that were in trouble, partly, at least, because the problems were the other guy's fault.

After we examined the systems that were in place to manage performance, it became apparent how this disconnection could exist. First, the majority of people did not feel that they benefited personally from the company's success. In this company, as in many others, the pay system was geared to meeting the external market and achieving internal equity. Thus, base pay depended on what people with similar skills and experience made elsewhere, and what people at similar levels of responsibility made within the company. Pay increases depended on individual merit as measured in the yearly performance appraisal, to which project performance was a negligible contributor. In fact, because there was a fixed pot of merit money, individuals saw themselves as being in competition with one another for their share of the pot. Second, although the individuals in this firm were clustered into interdisciplinary project teams, team performance was believed to contribute little to the reward and appraisal process. Indeed, the notion of team was an interesting one. In this company, teams were essentially large groups whose members had individual assignments that contributed to the project. Except for the top management, the team members did not really work together to accomplish a goal. The management met regularly to review the program, but team members reported that they received very little feedback on the status of the project. Thus, there was again a disconnection, this time between those who were *responsible* for the project and those who *did the work*.

In summary, the entire performance system in this company (and in many other companies as well) enabled, and indeed encouraged, individuals to see their own performance as separable from the enterprise as a whole. Individuals pursued their own assignments and were appraised and rewarded for how well they completed these assignments. In effect, each piece of a complex technical system was treated as a separate concept. Only managers possessed the information needed to fit the pieces together and to solve problems when the pieces didn't fit. Therefore, individuals disowned responsibility for the success of the final product.

One could almost say that certain behaviors were "locked in place" by the human resource systems. Risk taking was low, individuals worked in relative isolation, and the major concern in the company regarding pay was that people be treated equitably. To change this cycle would require major alterations in the goal-setting, decision-making, problem-solving, appraisal, and reward practices of the organization. In fact, this firm and many others are now engaged in such change. They are experimenting with systems that recognize the team as the unit of analysis. Goals have become team goals, problems are solved collectively, and individuals are appraised and rewarded, to a large extent, on how well the team meets its goal. Part of the reward still depends on how the business performed. Companies such as Motorola, Honeywell, McDonnell-Douglas, and TRW are the industry's leaders in this area.

In other industries, such companies as Lincoln Electric, Hewlett-Packard, and Donnelly Mirrors have long and successfully utilized various forms of profit-sharing and bonus incentive pay at the group level. Yet such approaches have not become the norm. There continues to be resistance in many quarters. Some of this reluctance has to do with assumptions about "what is right." We often hear the following or similar statements: We should not have to pay workers for good performance: that's like paying them extra to do their jobs. Or, It's really not feasible for workers to solve their own problems. All those meetings contribute to too much nonproductive time. That's why we pay managers.

From the early pioneers in this area, we have learned that it takes more than minor readjustment. In fact, every system of an organization must be examined. The opposition is intense and in some cases compelling. Individually based job design, performance appraisal, and reward systems have been developed by decades of work by industrial psychologists both within companies and within universities. Criteria of equity, validity, and individual motivational impact have been almost universally applied in evaluating these systems. Court cases regarding discrimination and unfair treatment are resolved on the basis of the same criteria. Thus, there is truly a formidable institutional barrier to change. However, it is encouraging that there is a crack in the edifice, and that there is now widespread experimentation with new systems. An alternative vision is beginning to develop, and approaches congruent with that vision are being forged (Lawler, 1986). More businesses appear to be facing the fact that they can no longer afford to separate their internal management systems from the final product.

The move to overcome this reluctance and make the transition is beginning to spread. A large number of companies have experimented with quality circles and other group problem-solving approaches. Other companies are seriously examining their technologies with an eye to redesigning work to facilitate teamwork. Frequently new plants are designed to promote teamwork and integration (Lawler, 1986).

Overcoming Inertia: What's Wakening the Sleeping Giants?

Perhaps nowhere are the needed changes more interesting and sweeping than in those organizations functioning for the first time in a deregulated environment. These include, among others, utilities and financial institutions. Historically these have been "sleeping giants" existing in a safe, predictable environment, regulated to ensure an unchallenged niche and a comfortable rate of return. Our comments in this section derive from experience with, primarily, the communications industry (formerly, the telephone companies). These organizations epitomize bureaucracy. Carrying the principle of standardization to an extreme, they are characterized by strong central control and standard operating procedures that rival those of the military. Layers of management monitor the work of the many classes of workers required to make these utilities function. All workers

receive enough training to do their prescribed jobs. Large centralized staff groups develop policies and procedures and revise
those policies when required. These organizations have, to a
large extent, been administered rather than managed. "Turf" is
jealously guarded and groups communicate as little as possible.
Personnel practices are very similar to those of civil service.

Through time, expensive duplication emerged as field
staff positions were created to help with local needs. Levels of
managers dealt with the substantial measuring and reporting required to meet engineered standards and headcounts. Meanwhile, they developed little sense of the overall business or
concern for optimizing resources. Profitability was not their responsibility. Change was cumbersome, as staff groups developed
uniform procedures for "rolling out" new programs and equipment, which in many cases had to be greatly modified to fit
local requirements.

These practices worked adequately in a protected environment. Regulatory commissions enabled costs to be passed on
to customers as rate hikes; an acceptable rate of return was
practically guaranteed. Deregulation and the computer revolution conspired to render such organizations obsolete. Suddenly,
the sleeping giants awakened to a competitive environment and
faced the challenges of achieving the agility necessary to implement technologies that radically altered the nature of the work
and of becoming profit oriented. Telephone company employees
were now required to sell services and products that changed
rapidly and worked according to new principles. "Equal access"
imposed new technical challenges and resulted in a clamor for
previously captive customers. The list of changes goes on. The
"telephone company" had to become a global competitor to
survive.

Similar upheaval occurred in other deregulated industries
as well. Airlines faced new competition for routes from small,
nonunionized companies, which often charged less for "no
frills" service. Electric companies faced competition from their
own customers. Deregulation of natural gas and huge swings in
the price of foreign oil caused major upheavals in oil and gas
companies. Banks faced competition from newcomers who were

prepared to provide new and different financial services (see Chapter Three). Companies everywhere were finding themselves playing new games by new rules, and for the first time employees were operating without the guidance of tested practices.

Many of these previously sleeping giants have begun to flex their muscle. They have broken up their monolithic structures, set up new divisions, and started new ventures. Internally, they have made systematic efforts at reeducation in an attempt to get managers to manage, to make profitability the primary concern, and to include risk taking and innovation as part of the organizational culture. Some companies have been almost ruthless in "downsizing" the structure. Other companies have struggled to align wages with reality, while making extensive capital investment in information technology, which is the nervous system of the enterprise.

Whether many of these companies survive the competitive shakeout remains to be seen. Those that do will no doubt emerge quite different from their original forms. Much of their success will depend on finding ways to address two imperatives that on the surface appear contradictory: first, to infuse the organization with initiative and innovation and, second, to successfully implement large-scale compatible systems that integrate all units and have specifications that permit minor local adaptation.

The challenge facing these companies is evolution of a new organizational form, one that houses the technical standardization necessary to permit worldwide information transfer and processing and yet fosters the creativity and flexibility necessary to adapt to ongoing change and to gain the competitive edge. People who fit the standardized system but who are innovative and creative and able to exist in a rapidly changing setting must be nurtured. A sense of responsibility for the success of the business must be generated at all levels of the organization, and yet the organization must focus huge investments that end up limiting local alternatives. Most important, these companies must introduce historically unprecedented change at a time when the realities of the economic environment are calling for efficiency and cost containment.

In the next section, we examine the strategies being utilized in adjusting to the global economy. Some of these strategies use new technical tools to enhance the efficiency or integration of work. Others challenge fundamental patterns of organization. Their goal is the creation of organizations in which people are aware of and able to meet the broad, diverse imperatives faced by business today.

Integration Within the Global Economy: Interesting Experiments

Electronics, aerospace and defense, utilities, financial services, and all other industries share a common threat to their traditional management practices: because of the major environmental changes discussed in Chapter Two, the slack is gone. Most companies face at least one of the following problems: increased global competition, upheaval caused by deregulation, an increasingly complex marketplace, and/or an economy with an increasingly systemic nature. In an article in *Fortune* magazine, Louis (1986) recently predicted that despite the overall economic upturns forecast for 1986 and beyond, companies should not expect these difficult conditions to disappear: "The competition between companies and between nations has grown fiercer, and the margin for error has shrunk. The changed economy demands shrewder management. In the seventies and early eighties, a manager could and often did get away with murder" (p. 35).

As more and more companies realize that survival is at stake, we see increasing trends toward bold experimentation with methods of management, which are described briefly in this section. These trends fall into two general categories: experiments that involve the internal organization and management of the company and experiments that transcend company boundaries and establish new economic relationships. Both trends challenge the assumptions and overturn the traditional constraints.

Trends which focus primarily on the internal functioning of the company include the following:

1. *Efforts to increase internal efficiency and effectiveness through changes in management style and focus.* Literally
hundreds of companies have invested heavily in efforts such as
employee involvement and quality processes. These efforts are
designed to involve members at all organizational levels in addressing work-related problems, reducing costs, improving quality, and improving work processes. Common to these approaches
is that *they leave the structure of the organization essentially
unaltered, but try to set in place processes of self-scrutiny and
norms of participation in self-improvement.* Thus, they have
challenged one fundamental assumption of the past—there is
one best way and the challenge of management is to find that
way and "put it in place."

2. *Efforts to make organizations "lean and mean."* Almost every company with which we come in contact has a version of this strategy in operation. Nationwide "downsizing" and
"levels and layers" analyses are in progress. Some organizations
became aware that they were significantly overstaffed; others
simply realized that they could not continue to operate com-
petitively without a significant decrease in wage burden. This
trend is not new. Indeed, one can say that it is cyclic in nature.
What is new is that in some cases it is leading to new concepts
of management. For example, many companies are beginning to
think in terms of a core of permanent workers with a fringe of
temporary workers. Although, historically, the layoff system
has achieved this state, it was applied primarily to blue-collar
workers. It has also been applied to contract white-collar workers and managers, primarily in such industries as aerospace, to
which large numbers of engineers have traditionally migrated.

There are definite human and societal costs to this downsizing trend. Questions of ethics arise when thousands of loyal,
long-term employees are put out on the streets. Is there no
other way to increase productivity and retain competitiveness?
Many companies have decided that the choice is between a stable, lean employment base and a continuation of old employment patterns with their ultimate threats to competitiveness
and survival. Will the long-term impact be fewer jobs for our
society or new forms of employment? Recently, a large num-

ber of companies in different industries have begun experimenting with hiring at least some of their expertise on a temporary, consulting basis. This turns on end traditional assumptions of what constitutes organizational membership, as well as the assumption that all needed skills should be housed internally. It opens new careers and brings into question the desirability of creating large hierarchies to house specialized groups.

3. *Efforts to redesign tasks.* Particularly in the manufacturing sector, companies are discovering that flat organizational structures composed of teams of employees can be clustered around manufacturing technologies in such a way that they can be largely self-managing with respect to a portion of the work flow. "Specialized" support tasks such as maintenance and quality assurance are often moved into the teams, as are many managerial and supervisory tasks. Such "new design" plants have been implemented in diverse industries, including oil and chemicals (Shell Sarnia), consumer goods (Procter & Gamble), industrial equipment (TRW, Cummins Engine), pharmaceuticals (Johnson & Johnson), semiconductors (DEC and Honeywell), and defense (Honeywell). These facilities overturn the traditional assumption that the role of management is to monitor the work of others and move responsibility to the people doing the work.

4. *Efforts to automate.* Recognizing the fact that management of new, more complex technologies requires different information systems, such companies as GM and Honeywell have developed single computerized networks that tie manufacturing systems together, thus integrating design, production, inventory, and quality control. These companies also plan to market their integrated manufacturing systems to other companies facing the same critical need.

In a related trend, a wide variety of companies are investing heavily in robotics, thus transferring repetitive precision jobs from hard-to-motivate workers to sophisticated machines. This trend is slowly transforming assembly-line work into process technology, where the job of the human worker becomes that of vigilance over machines, technical upkeep, and troubleshooting. Such companies as General Electric are finding that job

classifications must be changed in order to operate highly automated plants. "For the new plant to pay off . . . it must operate around the clock, seven days a week—necessitating a departure from traditional eight-hour work shifts and rigidly defined
job assignments" ("Swapping Work Rules for Jobs at G.E.'s
'Factory of the Future,' " 1984, pp. 43–46).

5. *Efforts to improve cooperation between labor and
management.* These are perhaps the most precarious of experiments. They involve challenging the assumptions and constraints concerning two institutions: business and labor. If the
mind set of management must be turned on end for it to see
labor as a partner in ensuring the success of the business, surely
no less is true for labor. For this reason, we see numerous companies choose to go it alone, using a wide variety of strategies to
place labor in the position of acquiescing or fighting to the bit-
ter end. Whatever the circumstances, it seems clear that the role
of labor is changing dramatically, and it is still too early to
know how that will settle out. Many companies realize that
they cannot make the transition without significant cooperation
from their work forces. Likewise, many labor unions realize that
entire industries and hundreds of thousands of jobs are at stake
in the effort to modernize. Thus, there have been a number of
bold ventures toward labor union/management cooperation in
addressing the challenges of the global economy. In the Decem-
ber 24, 1984, issue of *Business Week* Hoerr (1984) reported that
"Unions are now acting jointly with management in developing
new products and production technology, deciding on plant
location and organizing employee buyouts of failing companies
and plants" (p. 69). At Chrysler, we have seen union representation on the board of directors. At GM, we have seen the United
Auto Workers join management in the design of a new division
to produce the Saturn.

Perhaps the granddaddy of labor/management experiments is the Saturn project. It represents nothing less than a
total redesign of the factory as we have known it, utilizing all
of the approaches described above. Furthermore, it represents
a total departure from GM's traditional culture. Indeed, the
necessity to set up an entirely new division is a frank admission

that such an experiment could not be accomplished within GM's traditional organizational structure and culture.

The Saturn project represents a gigantic bet on the future of GM. The bet is that by setting up an entirely innovative organization, GM can cut the $2000- to $2500-per-unit gap between its production costs and those of its Japanese competitors. The Saturn unit will be an entirely separate division that will have been cooperatively designed by labor and management. It will incorporate a team-based management system and innovative personnel practices.

The Saturn project also represents a heavy bet on technology. It will house an entirely computerized information system that will collect, transmit, and keep track of the enormous amounts of information necessary to meet the following objectives: (1) to obtain the type of car and specific features desired by the consumer (this information will be entered into the system by the dealer in his showroom, thus saving on paperwork), (2) to send the order quickly to the factory where the car will be built without error or delay (this will reduce costs for GM because it will not be necessary to maintain a fixed inventory), and (3) to help the consumer arrange quicker and easier financing. To cut down on transportation and warehousing costs, production and assembly will occur in the same complex. "Even if Saturn doesn't succeed in completely closing the cost gap with the Japanese, the manufacturing technology that it is pioneering seems certain to take U.S. industrial productivity a giant step forward" (Whiteside and others, 1985, p. 128).

In addition to these and many other efforts to increase the effectiveness of internal organization, American businesses are experimenting with new ways of dealing with the business environment:

1. Ventures. Many companies are relying on the establishment of separate ventures and independent business units to develop and bring new technology and products to market. Thus, IBM established a separate business unit for initial work on its personal computer. Similarly, Apple Computer

housed the development of the Macintosh in a separate unit. AT&T is funding venture units with the explicit promise that they can depart from long-standing rules and procedures. 3M has created a career track and is providing funding for individuals who are able to build businesses. These ventures reflect the recognition that the ongoing inventiveness required to remain competitive may demand that young businesses be well funded and unencumbered by bureaucracy.

2. Collaborative relationships. A large number of joint ventures are being forged, as companies share resources and risks. In many cases these joint ventures span continents. Highly visible examples in the automobile industry include the GM/Toyota plant in Fremont, California, and GMF Robotics, the GM venture with Fanuc, a Japanese robot manufacturer.

To circumvent the high costs of domestic manufacturing, many companies are resorting to offshore manufacturing. High-technology companies such as Apple and Hewlett-Packard have invested heavily in manufacturing in the Far East. These ventures contribute to the trend toward increased globalization and cause some fear that American technological superiority may become a phenomenon of the past. In addition, domestic producers have almost totally withdrawn from some products, including calculators and video recorders.

Such companies as Caterpillar, General Electric, and Eastman Kodak practice "outsourcing," that is, buying components or finished products from overseas manufacturers that are then assembled and/or packaged and marketed under the domestic company's name. Companies are also forming close links with smaller, lower-cost domestic suppliers, in some cases positioning their own quality assurance and process engineering personnel in their suppliers' plants.

H. J. Heinz has even talked of giving up manufacturing and purchasing all products from companies with idle manufacturing capacity. This would enable Heinz to reduce its administrative structure substantially. If this is representative of a trend,

we may be seeing the beginning of a new organizational form
consisting of small central organizations that rely on a network
of external suppliers for manufacturing, distribution, marketing,
and billing. Such organizations have been referred to as "solar-
system organizations" by Piore and Sabel (1984) or simply as
network organizations.

The trends are clear. Although some companies are committed to one specific strategy, many are keeping their options
open. They are both strengthening their internal structures and
developing collaborative relationships with other companies.
Clearly, the organization that survives in the global economy
will be considerably different from past organizations.

The Hard Work Is Yet to Come

Although the organizations of the future are now at the
evolutionary stage, it's clear that they will differ substantially
from the large bureaucratic companies of the past. Emerging
organizations can be expected to tolerate greater *diversity* than
those of the past—ventures using different procedures, different
relationships with other companies, new career paths, and structures and roles that fit the technology of the unit. They can also
be expected to house a great deal of ongoing experimentation.

Tomorrow's organizations will be more *fluid,* conforming
less to standard procedures and more to the current needs of
the business or project. Temporary structures will become the
norm. Alliances will be forged on the basis of changing needs
and strategies. Boundaries within and between organizations
will become more permeable. Teamwork and communication
will provide the connectedness once afforded by a sense of
one's place in the structure. Leanness will be a prerequisite, as
an organization that is always ready to change cannot afford to
be weighted. The organizational infrastructure will be primarily
lateral, as networks develop among individuals, units, and organizations that are interdependent and require integration.

The organization of the future will be a demanding place
in which to work. Employees will need to have the big picture;
consequently, breadth as well as depth of skills and knowledge

will be required. There will be no such thing as a "safe career"; rather, there will be a need to grow and develop as the organization changes. Employees will have to develop notions of career that relate less to moving through a hierarchy and more to moving through a series of learning experiences. Organizations will become much more ambiguous to the people who occupy them.

In short, as we adjust to a global economy, we adjust to a more interconnected world. In such a world, organizations are not buffered from change, but rather are subjected to unpredictable change at a rapid rate. The only assumption that makes sense is that the requirements for success and the constraints on action will continue to change.

5

Correcting Tunnel-Vision Thinking and Facing the Threats to Our Long-Term Industrial Survival

"It is no accident... that work-force management in America has developed the way it has. The gradual evolution of a single, dominant paradigm for production and, for much of this century, the success it has enjoyed in the market have driven home to many managers the apparent validity of the assumptions upon which that paradigm was based. If skills can be progressively built into machines, then workers need not be especially skilled themselves. If a production system is to run economically, all considerations must be subordinated to the achievement of continuous high-volume operations. If costs creep up too far, turn up the pressure on workers or cut their pay or both. In short, follow the gospel of 'volume above all else' with an unblinking faith in its ultimate rightness, get skilled people out of the system wherever possible, automate everything in sight, gear up for long production runs, buffer yourself with enough inventory to keep the lines moving, inspect for defects—if at all—at the end of those lines, treat workers primarily as a reservoir of costs that can be bled out under pressure as the need arises, and you will boost your market share, your profits, your stockholders' good disposition, your bond ratings, your own compensation, and the nation's industrial health" (Abernathy and others, 1983, p. 91).

"The U.S. steel industry's underlying assumptions about the steel business prevented it from making the aggressive investments in modernization that were needed to match the pace of Japanese investment. From the U.S. company's point of view, the discounted cash flow return from a new low-cost . . . mill could not justify its construction. Levels of debt as high as [those] in the Japanese industry were unthinkable. Since no attempts were made to export in large quantities, growth rates were too slow to justify large additions to capacity. The investments the companies [made] . . . left the U.S. less competitive than [when] . . . modernization started" (Magaziner and Reich, 1983, pp. 165-166).

Executive Summary

Old Organizing Assumptions	*New Organizing Assumptions*
1. The fundamental structure (for example, competition, consumer tastes, technological and funding requirements) is basically stable and well understood.	1. Stability and complete knowledge of the fundamental structure can never be assumed.
2. Not only are customers loyal but their tastes are standardized.	2. The loyalty of consumers or the uniformity of their tastes cannot be taken for granted.
3. Nothing radically new will be invented that will alter fundamentally the nature of an industry's products.	3. Innovations that alter the entire shape of an industry may suddenly appear.
4. Innovations can be limited—for example, in the case of the auto industry, to driver comfort.	4. Limitation of innovation with respect to product design is industrial suicide.
5. Fundamental industrial practices shouldn't be changed until forced by	5. Serious change should be anticipated and actively championed.

Old Organizing Assumptions	*New Organizing Assumptions*
competition or governmental edicts. Major energy should be focused on resistance to change.	
6. Innovation can take a back seat to efficiency.	6. Efficiency and innovation are both important. Without innovation, efficiency doesn't count for much.
7. Neither managers nor workers need to understand the entire production process. Quality products can be produced by those with a limited vision and understanding of their jobs.	7. Both managers and workers need to see the big picture if they are to be motivated to produce quality products.

In certain key respects, individual companies are like individual people. In Western societies, at least, individuals are supposed to exist independently; that is, each person is responsible for his or her actions and is recognized apart from the larger social fabric. In the strict sense, this is impossible. We are all part of the larger social collective from which we derive a fundamental sense of identity, meaning, and belonging. Thus, individual companies are more like the members of a family. Neither the individual members nor the entire family can exist or be recognized apart from each other. We are just beginning to realize that what has taken family therapists decades to learn, namely, that one can successfully neither diagnose nor treat "truly sick" members of a family without diagnosing and treating the whole family, applies to industry as well.

To understand an industry, it is not enough, for instance, as in Chapter Three, to recognize the assumptions that made for General Motors's (GM's) "failure of success." If one company has a set of rarely articulated, deep beliefs that guides its behavior, then the industry must also have a set of rarely articulated, deep beliefs that guides its behavior. Studying these basic beliefs helps us to gain insight into the changes required to revitalize American industry and to compete successfully on the world scene.

The job of understanding any industry is so horrendous and complex that it is doubtful it could be accomplished in a single book, let alone chapter. The job of understanding and comparing whole industries is even more difficult. Our task thus seems doomed from the outset, and it is, depending on what we mean by "understanding" and "comparison."

In this chapter, we want primarily to understand and to compare two industries, automobile and steel. It should be obvious why we choose these industries. They are two of our oldest, most basic manufacturing industries. One, the automobile, has a real chance of making a comeback; the other, steel, does not. Thus, if we can learn what went wrong with both and, further, why one seems capable of turning things around, then we can begin to form a bigger picture of what's required of all industries to survive in today's globally competitive world. In short, we can use these industries as a baseline in comparisons of other industries.

One way in which we made this task more manageable was to reduce the excellent, but by now overwhelming, volumes of studies (Abernathy, 1983; Lawrence and Dyer, 1983; Scott and Lodge, 1985) to two tables. These two tables, one for each industry, summarize our research and our experience in consulting with individual companies. Each table lists approximately twenty key assumptions. We do not contend that these tables capture all the nuances of these industries. We would be absurd to think they could. What we do contend is something quite different. These tables provide insight into the many factors responsible for the paths that both industries followed. More important, they provide a potent way of examining the status of any industry, because they zero in on the essentials.

Because of the critical nature of our examination, a few qualifications are necessary before we present our findings. Many, if not most, of the assumptions were never fully or explicitly articulated, and certainly not in the form in which we have stated them. Most were implicit in the behavior and poli-

cies of the industries as they developed. Indeed, in many cases
they can be gleaned clearly only from the vantage point of the
present. Further, the reader must be warned that each assumption is worded as an "absurd proposition," as discussed in Chapter Three, not only because what was reasonable in earlier times
is now absurd, but because we deliberately worded each proposition to make its absurdity clear. Actually, we have supplied
two wordings. The first, or "generic" rule, is our "no holds
barred" translation of what we take to be or to have been the
underlying spirit of the assumption governing a particular aspect
of the industry. The second, or "historic" rule, is closer to the
neutral or scholarly wording as it appears, in some cases almost
verbatim, in the academic literature.

Finally, it must be strictly understood that if we seem
overly critical of both industries it is only because we want to
learn to avoid similar mistakes in the future. We doubt that anyone would have acted differently at the time these two industries were born and developed. But the nature of worldwide
competition today is such that we can no longer afford to ignore these mistakes.

The Glorious Birth, Maturity,
Decline, and Hopeful Signs of Rebirth
of the American Car Industry

Table 3 lists what we take as the principal assumptions
that guided the American automobile industry from its birth.
We would not have the confidence we do in reducing the complexity and long history of the industry to a limited number of
assumptions were it not for some brief, essential facts. First, the
same basic themes emerge repeatedly from all major accounts
of the history and nature of the industry. Second, in many
cases, the general tone of these accounts is as strong and as critical as the "generic rules" and, in some cases, more critical
(Abernathy, 1983; Lawrence and Dyer, 1983; Scott and Lodge,
1985; Yates, 1984).

The earliest years of the American automobile industry
were marked by intense competition between many small firms,

Table 3. The Unwritten Rules of the U.S. Automobile Industry.

	Generic Rule		Historic Rule
1.	An easy, short childhood is the best preparation for adulthood and maturity.	1.	It is a distinct advantage that by about 1930 the modern automobile industry was firmly established, its competitive practices well understood, its major product design features firmly locked into place, and so on.
2.	We are stable now and forevermore; the broader world is stable.	2.	The competitive dynamics and basic business of automobile production are essentially stable and well known.
3.	"They love us" (that is, our products); they're loyal, won't switch; we can take them for granted; we can assume consumer stability.	3.	The tastes of U.S. car buyers are standardized and stable; thus, except for yearly style changes, we do not have to make radical or substantial changes in our product; U.S. car buyers will not demand a new type of car.
4.	Nothing new will be invented that will radically shake up our product; we essentially know it all; the stability of car technology can be taken for granted.	4.	The design/production of future cars will not require fundamentally new manufacturing processes or technologies.
5.	Our focus need not be broader than the driver; a restricted focus of innovation can be assumed.	5.	Innovations relating to driver comfort are more important than fundamental technical innovations.
6.	Don't change until forced to; resist, deny change; put your major energies into denial and resistance.	6.	We can succeed by not spending money on fundamental innovations until forced by governmental regulatory agencies, foreign competition, consumers, and others.
7.	Get your priorities wrong; innovation can take a back seat to efficiency.	7.	Because of GM's dominant industry strategy (under A. P. Sloan) based on clever marketing to different demographic segments of the population and frequent style changes, technical innovation is subordinate to efficiency in production; that is, efficiency is more important than innovation.

(continued on next page)

Table 3. The Unwritten Rules of the U.S. Automobile Industry, Cont'd.

	Generic Rule		Historic Rule
8.	Keep getting your priorities wrong; good labor relations can take a back seat to efficiency.	8.	Efficiency in production is more important than good labor relations; good labor relations are not important to efficiency.
9.	We're so big and powerful, smug, and secure that we can shut out the whole world; we can charge and pass on to our customers anything we want; so what if we're arrogant?	9.	Foreign competition will never be significant; therefore, U.S. carmakers will not be prevented from passing the higher production costs necessary to keep up with the competition on to consumers.
10.	Since we don't need much innovation, we can finance whatever we want to.	10.	The capital and debt capacity required to finance the required innovations are readily available.
11.	Managers don't need challenge in their work; the restricted focus/nature of managerial work can be assumed.	11.	As the business of car making becomes well understood, managerial work becomes routine and it is desirable that it become so; challenge in managerial work is not necessary to the long-term success of the industry.
12.	If you want tunnel vision, then you have to reward it; we are masters at creating a system for producing managerial myopia.	12.	An extremely handsome bonus system that rewards top management for short-term thinking is not hazardous to the long-term interests of the industry.
13.	Workers don't need challenge in their jobs; the restricted focus/nature of all jobs can be assumed.	13.	Workers are willing to trade money for challenge in their jobs.
14.	Keep everyone small-minded and uninvolved.	14.	It is not necessary to involve most employees in the larger purposes of the business.
15.	Don't rock the boat; don't bite the hand that feeds you.	15.	It is not in the interests of top management to tamper with the system that has promoted them; it is not necessary for top management to look at the big picture.

16. We don't need the constant informal parties they do in Silicon Valley.

17. We've discovered *the* principles of organization for all time.

18. No one, including ourselves, can teach us anything about good organization.

16. It is not necessary to breed/foster an industrywide culture of innovation, intense competition, informal sharing of information, entrepreneurialism, and intense cycling of executives.

17. The organizational structure of U.S. carmakers is not only appropriate for its time, if not all time, but is well suited to responding to changing governmental policies, consumer tastes, and foreign competition.

18. Despite GM's great success, due to its early organizational structure under Alfred P. Sloan, Ford has been correct in resisting the professionalization of its upper management for so long, and Chrysler has been correct in resisting adoption of GM's structure of high differentiation and high integration; in other words, U.S. carmakers have nothing significant to learn from one another regarding the design of their organizational structures.

often no more than homespun businesses, typical of most industries in their beginning, or "start-up," phase. Thus, by 1900
there were some 58 "firms," if they could be called that, selling
"cars." By 1910, there were more than 200 such start-ups.

The reasons for the explosion in start-ups are not hard to
fathom. The basic costs of assembling a car were low. Almost
anyone could scrape together the small amounts of capital required to assemble a car in a backyard garage. As the industry
grew rapidly, it became impossible for some of these small
firms to remain in business. For instance, by 1908, the top
three producers—Ford, GM, and Studebaker (which then marketed under the name EMF)—accounted for approximately 50
percent of the United States's total production of cars. By the
end of the 1920s, the seven largest firms accounted for more
than 90 percent of the market.

Long-term survival, however, was another matter, as the
novelty of early cars began to wear off. As a result, nearly all of
the early start-ups have long since ceased to exist. Their names,
however, still beckon us back to an earlier, simpler era: Stanley
Brothers, General Electric, Maytag, Sears, and Harvard. The reasons for the shakeout are also not hard to understand. One, a
recession in 1920 and 1921 wiped out most small firms. Two,
the overall demand for cars dropped off sharply in the 1920s so
that carmakers found themselves in strong competition for the
same customers. Three, with their decisively greater economies
of scale achieved through mass production, the larger firms
could offer larger sedans at lower prices.

Perhaps what in the long run proved most decisive was
that by about 1930 the basic structure of the entire industry
had been established. The addition of automatic transmissions
in the 1940s completed the basic design that would dominate
the industry for thirty years. The major firms competed mainly
on the basis of styling and amenities such as dealer service, and
not on the basis of technology. American cars became synony-
mous with bigness, luxury, and comfort.

Given the basic design, it cost as much to produce a big
bolt as it did to produce a small bolt. And by extrapolation, it
cost as much to produce a big car as it did to produce a small
car. However, the profits on big cars were considerably greater

than those on small cars because, psychologically, customers would spend more for big cars. Further, gasoline was essentially cheap during this period. Therefore, both the industry and the consumers became addicted to a product that was suited, at best, to only one very special set of conditions that had lasted so long as to make them seem natural and enduring. It was not true then, and certainly is not true today, that big cars are more profitable to produce than small cars. Rather, the industry was locked into manufacturing processes and factories that favored the production of big cars as opposed to small cars.

World War II only reinforced the implicit biases of the industry. The market after World War II was essentially a seller's market. Consumers were hungry for cars and hence gobbled up anything thrown at them. Further, the internal domestic market was so large that for all essential purposes the market for American cars was the entire United States. Therefore, the U.S. car companies could ignore the rest of the world, a theme that we explored in more depth in Chapter Two.

The preceding discussion provides background and testimony to at least the first ten assumptions in Table 3. The intent of the assumptions should be clear. Only one might conceivably require modification: if the "early childhood" of the U.S. auto industry with its intense competition and recessions was not as easy as Assumption 1 makes it appear, then certainly the "teen" or "early adult" years were. Once the survivors made it past the trauma of birth, they were virtually assured of immortality, or so it seemed for some forty to fifty years. Now, although forty to fifty years is insignificant from the standpoint of geological history, it is long from the standpoint of an individual's lifetime within a particular industry. As we have painfully learned, forty to fifty years is more than enough time to instill the conditions for the "failure of success." As Abernathy and his colleagues (1983) put it, "The market for automobiles after World War II was a seller's market and the domestic producers flourished. Increases in costs were readily passed along to the consumer, whose appetite for fins, chrome, and horsepower appeared insatiable. Success bred success and confirmed the managerial decisions responsible for it" (p. 46).

The U.S. auto industry did more than ignore the rest of

the world. It believed that its internal markets were invulnerable
to penetration by the outside world (Assumption 9). In addition, other partially articulated assumptions supported their
position: (1) We're shielded from imports ever gaining a significant toehold in the U.S. market because (2) the rest of the
world can't establish the domestic dealer outlets and support
networks for parts, service, and financing that we've established
over the years. As did all assumptions of the industry, these
proved false as well during the 1970s and 1980s, for example,
when Volkswagen not only produced a car that was fun and
economical to drive ("the bug"), but quickly established, to the
dismay of domestic producers, an elaborate dealer network
which offered high-quality service and customer support.

If forty to fifty years is a long time in the history of an
industry, then ten years is a short time for the basic character of
an industry to change. Indeed, it feels as if almost overnight the
entire character of the U.S. auto industry, if not that of the industry worldwide, has changed completely. Where once all cars
were oriented toward bigness, comfort, and luxury, they now
are oriented toward fuel efficiency, quality of construction, and
reliability of operation and maintenance. To achieve success in
today's market one must combine low price with high performance and quality. The change is thus so fundamental that it
has taken what seems an inordinate amount of time for Detroit
to realize that today's cars are an entirely different breed and
respond. Wedded to old ways, some in Detroit will have not gotten the message and probably never will. The reasons can be
found in assumptions 11 through 18 in Table 3.

Building an entirely new kind of car demands more than
a different attitude toward innovation, technology, plants,
equipment, and financing. It also demands the development of
entirely new attitudes about workers, middle managers, and
even top managers. The Japanese have learned one essential lesson: *it is impossible to build good-quality products without
quality work relationships.* The active participation and deep
understanding of both labor and management are required for

the entire manufacturing process. This means that both workers and managers must be involved in every phase of design, manufacture, and marketing. As Abernathy and his colleagues (1983) stated so well, "the work force must be viewed as something to be nurtured, not as an impersonal, inanimate 'thing' which is merely bought and sold" (p. 78). To achieve this end, however, to view labor and even management in a different light, the long, horrible history of poor relations between labor and management in the automobile industry must be overcome.

As we discussed in Chapter Four, changing any human system, whether it be an individual firm or a whole industry, demands changing a number of factors. We argued that at least six key variables are involved in the design and operation of any organization: (1) rewards, (2) information, (3) tasks, (4) people, (5) structure, and (6) organizational culture. The Japanese have learned how to deal with all of these variables at once. For instance, they have learned that to build a better car one must visualize as many of the problems that will compromise its quality as possible. This means establishment of an organization that recruits, trains, and *rewards* its members for uncovering and solving problems, not hiding them. Attention to only the short term and ignorance of the big picture can't be rewarded.

If one looks at all eighteen assumptions in Table 3, one finds that they fall into distinct groups. First, the industry naively and wrongly assumed that because it was born and grew to maturity in relatively easy circumstances, it would always exist in relative comfort. It mistook an accidental circumstance of history for a natural and permanent occurrence. In short, it made a false assumption with regard to continuity of the external environment: *things always will be good because they always have been.* Second, the industry took for granted the loyalty of its consumer base and the unchangeability of consumer tastes. It thus made a highly critical assumption regarding its primary stakeholder, customers. Third, the industry minimized the need for constant innovation, and its adoption into the working design of cars, until it was forced upon it by foreign competition. It thus made an assumption with regard to both its primary stakeholder, that is, customers would be satisfied with whatever they were given, and another important stakeholder, that is, foreign competition would never be powerful. Fourth, it assumed that labor and management, two other important stakeholders, did not need jobs that challenged them and forced them to see the big picture. As a result, fifth, it is not surprising that both parties assumed they could shut out the rest of the world, thus narrowing their vision. Sixth, both labor and management assumed that if the basic design of cars was fixed, the traditional, hierarchical, bureaucratic structure needed to produce them should be, too. They thus made a critical assumption about the kind of organizational structure needed to manufacture cars. Finally, seventh, the members of the industry basically assumed that they could neither learn from one another regarding basic organization design nor gain from intense competition.

The result was extreme isolation from the rest of the world, a cocoonlike mentality and existence—tunnel vision of the worst kind (Yates, 1984). Thus, whether it intended to or not, the industry had in effect concocted a system that prevented it from learning about both the outside world and its inside world. It even went so far as to handsomely reward workers and managers for being myopic.

The very rationale for the existence of such systems becomes the denial of external warning signs that signal an abrupt change in the outside world (Yates, 1984). Such systems perpetuate their own closed view of reality and, therefore, are nearly, but not completely, impossible to change. For these reasons, mild shocks or portents of change are not sufficient to induce a response. The signals must be massive and sustained if they are to break down the wall of self-perpetuating unreality that has built up over the years. Thus, the earnings of the major American automobile companies not only had to go into the red but had to stay in the red for several quarters before the message got through to executives and workers that things were never going to return to normal. Both managers and workers had built a system for living in the short term. They had to be hit in the only place it would be felt, that is, in short-term measures of performance, the bottom line. The handsome bonuses of top executives had to dry up and the jobs of workers had to be threatened on a previously unknown scale.

At the end of Chapter Four, we showed that there are signs that the U.S. auto industry has gotten the message that the assumptions by which it has lived are no longer appropriate and it is actively attempting to reverse the old order. GM's Saturn experiment is highly significant in this respect because it is based on the complete reversal of every assumption in Table 3. Once an organization has moved into the outer reaches of the A region, signaled by the collapse of its major operating assumptions, its only salvation is a program of organizational renewal based on the deliberate and systematic abandonment of the old assumptions. It has no choice. And it can't do it piecemeal or timidly. It's got to embrace change dramatically and boldly. The lesson for the United States, and the world, is that the automobile industry is never going back to what it was. Therefore, we predict, regardless of whether it succeeds, that Saturn will be a stepping-stone to the survival of the entire industry. Indeed, it's called an "experiment" because no one knows whether it will succeed. One experiments to learn.

Finally, for an entire industry to learn and to change, most of the firms in that industry must experiment simultaneously. Otherwise, the new culture of innovation will not take hold. Thus, it is not enough that one company experiment (GM with Saturn); other companies must do so as well. There is evidence that such is the case. Both Ford and Chrysler have demonstrated their versions of the GM strategy in buying electronic information companies to help automate their factories to cut manufacturing costs; both are also experimenting with different compensation and profit-sharing plans to motivate workers and managers to see the big picture, to promote involvement, and to provide a real incentive to cut costs and increase profits. Combined with these motives is a concern for international competitiveness through a greater emphasis on quality.

The Birth, Maturity, and Decline
of the U.S. Steel Industry

Unlike the U.S. auto industry, the U.S. steel industry does not show signs of recovery. The steel industry appears permanently trapped in its outmoded view of the world—in its outdated assumptions.

There is no need to detail the history of the steel industry. Although its history is not identical to that of the auto industry, the preceding discussion together with the following passages from Magaziner and Reich (1983) are more than sufficient to provide the necessary brief background to interpret the assumptions in Table 4:

In the 1950s, U.S. steelmakers produced almost 50 percent of the world's steel. They had the world's largest, most efficient steel-producing facilities. While the U.S. had the world's highest wage rates, it was the world's lowest-cost producer of steel, and the world's largest exporter. The combination of high productivity and access to good, low-cost raw materials gave the U.S. a significant competitive advantage. Today, the U.S. produces only 16 percent of the total world steel output and exports less than one-tenth of the amount exported by the Japanese. Imports took over 18 percent of U.S. consumption of steel in 1978 before barriers were erected to limit them.

Declining productivity in the steel industry has had a wide-ranging impact. U.S. producers of automobiles, appliances, ships, and other steel-using products have been put at a serious disadvantage by having to buy higher-priced American steel. In 1977 and 1978, companies manufacturing cars in the U.S. had to pay 25 to 30 percent more for their steel than did their Japanese counterparts [p. 155].

U.S. steel companies made small, incremental investments to obtain "cheap" capacity rather than make the larger, more aggressive, and riskier investments that could have led to superior productivity overall. In fact, because of its high capital costs, the Bethlehem Steel plant at Burns Harbor, Indiana, was long viewed as unprofitable, even though it is the only fully integrated large-scale greenfield plant built in the U.S. since 1952. Overall, U.S. steel companies have sought to keep the return on investment—ROI—up by keeping the "I" low, but this strategy has left whole plants uncompetitive. In the long run this scheme has been self-defeating [p. 161].

During the early 1970s, lack of understanding of market development and of competitors was a serious problem in the U.S. steel industry. A reasonably small circle of "industry experts" and company leaders had set up a fairly insulated and mutually reinforcing mythology about the strength of the American steel industry and the vulnerability of the Japanese steel industry, if stripped of its "unfair trade practices." Business leaders spent too much time worrying about unfair trading and the need to diversify investments instead of planning investments to reassert technological and productivity leadership [p. 164].

Inspection of Tables 3 and 4 reveals that they are essentially the same. One is reminded of Tolstoy's famous saying that all happy families are alike in their happiness but that each family is unhappy in its own distinct way. Nevertheless, there must be subtle differences if the auto industry has a chance, however debatable, of recovering, but the steel industry appears to have lost its chance. As we see it, two outstanding differences exist. First, no leader of stature who has staked his company's

Table 4. The Unwritten Rules of the U.S. Steel Industry.

	Generic Rule		*Historic Rule*
1.	Steel is a simple business.	1.	Steel making is and always will be a straightforward, that is, noncomplex, business.
2.	Steel is and always will be a good business.	2.	Favorable environmental operating conditions for the steel industry are permanent.
3.	Because of the essentially simple nature of our business, there's essentially just one way to organize.	3.	Highly centralized, functional, bureaucratic organizational structures are appropriate for steel companies because of the straightforward nature of their business.
4.	An easy childhood is the best preparation for adulthood and maturity.	4.	The relatively placid environment into which the industry was born and the subsequent stability of that environment are favorable to the long-term survival of the industry.
5.	The best way to face the future is by looking back and staying rooted in the past.	5.	The best way to protect the industry is to freeze production and investments at past levels; that is, the best policies for the industry to pursue are defensive, reactive strategies based on the past.
6.	We're so big and powerful, smug, and secure that we can shut out the whole world; the rest of the world isn't even worth a fight.	6.	The industry can be successful by concentrating only on domestic markets; conversely, the industry can afford to give up foreign markets without much of a sacrifice.
7.	We're so big and powerful we might as well just be one company anyway.	7.	The essential dominance of one company, the U.S. Steel Company, is good for the entire industry.
8.	We're OK; everyone else is not OK; get the outside world off our backs; who do they think they are?	8.	Misfortunes are due primarily to outside forces, for example, unfair trade practices, government interference, high labor costs.
9.	Fight outsiders to the death; never give an inch.	9.	It is important to spend considerable time and money fighting government policies that one has little hope of changing instead of seeking compromises with those policies and learning how to adjust.
10.	Avoid, deny, and resist instead of adapt, learn, and mature.	10.	Crises can be met successfully through strategies of crisis avoidance, for example, through diversification and mergers, instead of through fundamental organizational innovation.

11. We don't need to learn how to produce more efficiently.

12. Since we don't need to learn how to produce more efficiently, we don't need any competition to prod us.

13. We don't need to strive for excellence generally; conversely, we can get by with restricted excellence.

14. Bigger is more important than quality in innovation.

15. Bet your money on the past and present, not on the future.

16. Invest small in innovation; don't borrow to invest in innovation.

17. Keep everyone small-minded and uninvolved; tunnel vision is the best policy for everyone.

18. Everyone can have any job they want as long as it's at the bottom.

19. No one else has anything new to teach us.

20. Stay put; we practice not-invented-here by deliberate intention and careful planning.

11. Maximizing the efficiency of production is not necessary to the long-term survival of the industry.

12. The level and type of competition that would force the maximization of efficiency is not necessary to the long-term survival of the industry.

13. It is not necessary to pursue excellence in either innovation or efficiency.

14. Increasing the volume of total steel production by building larger manufacturing plants is more important than introducing newer, possibly smaller, steel plants that feature revolutionary steel-making techniques; that is, volume is more important than innovation.

15. Investment capital should be spent mainly, if not solely, on the expansion of existing plants rather than on cost-saving innovations.

16. Required innovations can be financed solely through internal funds.

17. It is not necessary for either top management or union leadership to involve the work force in the larger issues of the industry.

18. Rigid, traditional patterns of recruitment, that is, essentially one entry-level position at the bottom, are acceptable.

19. It is not necessary to recruit potential managers at the major schools of business or to bring in outside managers.

20. Top managers are expected to spend their entire careers in one company.

entire fortunes on an experiment of the magnitude of Saturn,
has emerged in the steel industry. No leader in the steel industry seems willing to make the type of investment required to
buy a Hughes aircraft company, as GM did to provide the
technological infrastructure necessary to support Saturn. Or,
to put it slightly differently, to survive today, industry requires strong leadership to challenge and reverse the assumptions on which it was founded. Second, to challenge is not
enough. The challenged assumptions must be replaced in a way
that is clearly visible to all; otherwise, the entire effort will
merely remain academic. That's why concrete, highly visible,
and significant experiments are vital. They not only make the
new order of things visible but also demonstrate the commitment of the organization. Surfacing and challenging one's old
assumptions without a concrete design in which to ground the
new assumptions is a sterile and empty intellectual exercise at
best. On the other hand, designing and executing a concrete experiment without challenging past assumptions can be narrow
and shortsighted, that is, not well thought out and hence not
well suited to what's required.

We believe that the conclusions we have derived from the
preceding examination, however brief, generalize to all industries. Although industries differ greatly in the nature of their
products, their organizational characteristics, their capital and
information requirements, their dealer support systems, and so
on, they share two principles essential for survival in today's
environment: (1) clear recognition and understanding of the
role that past assumptions have played in operations and (2)
continuous experimentation with new organizational forms for
introducing and adopting innovations. Those industries that
clearly understand these two principles will survive; those that
do not, will not.

It should be noted that these two principles apply irrespective of the size of individual firms within an industry. Thus,
if the U.S. steel industry does survive, it will probably do so
because of the growth of new, small firms, not old, large firms
such as the U.S. Steel Company. The newer firms have discov-

ered their niche by producing specialty steels. They also have incorporated the latest steel-producing technology in mini mills and have an entirely different understanding of the needs of their employees. In short, it appears that they are succeeding by reversing the assumptions in Table 4.

As we indicated at the beginning of the chapter, we cannot assess the chances for survival of every industry in the United States. We can, however, point to a few industries and, by showing how they are faring with regard to our two principles, evaluate their chances for survival.

It appears that the U.S. health care industry will survive, but only because it has undergone a major transformation. Those who have studied this industry know that methods of health care and delivery have changed radically since 1980 (Arnold, 1985; Diamond, 1985; Kraft, 1985; Moreland, 1985; Nelson, 1985; Nelson and Roark, 1985; Peterson, 1985; Shiver, 1985; Starr, 1982). Once the medical profession was tightly controlled by individual doctors and medical associations; in a few short years control has all but shifted to huge health care conglomerates. It is predicted that all independent practitioners, except highly skilled specialists, will disappear in the next few years. What was the triggering event? The astronomically rising costs of medical care. Actually, it was the U.S. government in the form of Medicare benefits that put an end to the traditional behavior of doctors and hospitals. The medical profession had made the critical assumption that it was exempt from the normal laws of economics because of the special nature of medicine. Indeed, the government said that as of a certain date, it would pay only fixed fees for medical practices. As a result, those doctors and hospitals that knew how to play the game only in terms of "open-ended costs" found themselves no longer able to survive within the new rules or, in our language, the new assumptions. The winners were those who knew how to deliver health care *for profit within the "constraints" of the new game* (Arnold, 1985; Diamond, 1985; Kraft, 1985; Moreland, 1985; Nelson, 1985; Nelson and Roark, 1985; Peterson, 1985; Shiver, 1985; Starr, 1982). (The jury is still out on whether this can be done for all segments of the population; the

fear is that the rich will receive quality health care at an affordable cost and the poor will receive minimal care and at an un-
affordable cost.)

Thus, the health care industry has clearly recognized the
fact that the old assumptions are outmoded. In addition, it has
initiated new organizational experiments, such as health maintenance organizations (HMOs), to deliver health care financed in
a different way. What is so fascinating to us is that some of
these organizational experiments embody some of the innovations in GM's Saturn project. For instance, Humana Hospital,
one of the largest HMOs in the United States, if not the world,
is placing a computer terminal beside the bed of every patient
(Keppel, 1985). Humana's purpose, like that of GM in locating
computer terminals in dealers' showrooms in the Saturn experiment, is to reduce labor costs by cutting the expenses involved
in storing, retrieving, and updating the tremendous amounts of
information connected with running a hospital. Here, once
again, we see the critical role that information is playing today.

No discussion would be complete without mention, however brief, of two successful industries that have played a central role in the development of this nation's economy: agriculture and housing (Lawrence and Dyer, 1983; Vogel, 1985). A
cursory examination reveals once again the critical role that assumptions play in the health of an industry over its lifetime.
Furthermore, the idea of a significant organizational experiment
as central to an industry's survival takes on new meaning through
an examination of these industries.

As different as agriculture and housing are, they nonetheless share common features. One, by nature, both businesses are
extremely cyclical, in part because of geography and climate,
and in part because of their dependence on other parts of the
economy; for example, in both industries, changes in interest
rates greatly affect the borrowing patterns of both producers
and consumers. Because of the large geographic, climatic, and
economic variations, both industries have long held the tenet
(that is, the critical assumption) that the construction of single-
family homes and farming are best practiced by small family

firms. Their assumption is that economies of scale obtainable in other industries are not possible for them. The consequence is a constraint on the kinds of organizational experiments possible. If conventional wisdom in both industries is to be believed, nothing akin to a large-scale Saturn project seems possible. It should not be concluded that major organizational experiments have not been undertaken. On the contrary, as commentators have pointed out, the agriculture industry in particular would not have achieved the success it has were it not for the extensive role played by the U.S. government, mainly through the Department of Agriculture. Indeed, the U.S. government has supported nearly every aspect of farming: education concerning modern agriculture practices, mass dissemination of innovations, and, perhaps most important, extensive financial support in the form of subsidies and tariffs.

That these industries have been in serious trouble for some time is common knowledge. Their dispersed nature makes the choice of an appropriate organizational experiment difficult at this time. Proposals are not entirely lacking—for example, complete withdrawal of all farm price supports. What's seriously lacking, in our opinion, is reform based on our two principles: (1) systematic analysis of the key assumptions upon which the industry is based and (2) far-reaching organizational experiments based on challenge of the original assumptions. We have constantly stressed the importance of these two principles throughout this and previous chapters because of the critical role that assumptions play in social life. Assumptions constitute the foundation upon which human activity rests. Assumptions constitute the social glue that holds everything together. Given their importance, it is all the more shocking to find that in this country, virtually no major associations systematically track the assumptions upon which a particular industry is based and look for signals, however weak, that undermine those assumptions. Perhaps the task has been neglected because it is so basic. In our view, it is critical to survival.

We are constantly told that we need to collect more information if we are to master a world that grows increasingly complex. We disagree strongly. We don't need more information; we need less noise. To paraphrase Russell L. Ackoff (1981), to manage effectively in a global economy does not require endless amounts of relevant information; it requires less irrelevant information.

6

Organizing at the National Level for More Effective Global Competitiveness

"Our ability to respond to the new international competitive environment is the paramount problem of our generation, and a successful response may well provide the paramount opportunity for national renaissance. . . .

". . . How many more industries must America lose to convince those who believe that yen revaluation and correct monetary and fiscal policies are enough to solve our problems? How large does the trade imbalance have to become? How much of the high-tech market and service sector must America lose before it gives up the ideological pretense that the private sector is able to respond effectively if just left alone? What could leaders do to increase public awareness of the underlying problems?" (Vogel, 1985, p. 271).

"Japan's Ministry of International Trade and Industry provides business with a *"vision"* (note, not a *"plan"*) of where the economy could best be directed in the national interest [italics ours]. The efforts of it and other agencies no doubt help explain the general acceptance by the Japanese public that as some industries grow and flourish others must in the nature of things languish and decline. There seems to be no other nation in the world where even relatively low-ranking bureaucrats can with impunity publicly list industries that will and must phase out of the economy.

"With all of these strengths it is critical to the economic growth process that the government of Japan sees, as it does, the private company as the necessary, effective, and appropriate instrument for the nation's economic development. When this policy view by government is coupled with a perception by the business community of the government as generally competent and supporting, a degree of government-business dialogue and cooperation becomes possible that is rare in the West" (Abegglen and Stalk, 1985, pp. 31-32).

Executive Summary

Old Organizing Assumptions	*New Organizing Assumptions*
1. The basic problem underlying the United States's lack of competitiveness in world markets is fundamentally economic in nature.	1. The basic problem is fundamentally structural, that is, economic *and* organizational.
2. Hence, such traditional solutions as devaluation of the dollar and yen, balancing of huge federal deficits, lowering of trade barriers, and implementation of tax incentives to stimulate investment are still appropriate and all that is needed.	2. Hence, solutions that reframe old ideas within new contexts are required. The United States must design new social institutions, as have the other countries with which we compete, to fashion coordinated economic policies.
3. The United States does not need a coordinated economic or industrial policy (IP). The free market is still the best mechanism for running a complex society. Influence, coordina-	3. The United States has always had an IP by fiat through the innumerable tax breaks, favorable loans, and protective laws that helped launch and sustain all of the major in-

Old Organizing Assumptions   *New Organizing Assumptions*

tion, or orchestration is equivalent to government control or centralized planning.

dustries. The United States can no longer follow an IP that has evolved in a haphazard uncoordinated fashion. The free market is more of a myth than a reality in today's world; orchestration is not and need not be equivalent to control.

4. Even if an IP were desirable, it would be impossible to administer because the agency that would formulate and implement it would be fatally undermined by traditional bureaucratic and political forces.

4. Traditional bureaucratic and political forces are a serious problem. There is no guarantee that they can be overcome, but if they cannot, we will be uncompetitive. The experience of other countries shows that in principle it is possible to design new mechanisms *if* we have the desire to do it.

The thesis of this book is that at every level of society we require new, imaginative forms of organization if we are to meet the challenges of global competition. In Chapter Three, we argued that individuals need to think differently to respond to these challenges. In Chapters Four and Five, we argued that individual firms and entire industries, respectively, need to reorganize to promote teamwork at all levels.

In this chapter, we continue our theme of radical reorganization. We argue that we cannot meet the challenge of an interconnected world by confining changes to individuals, firms, and industries. New kinds of institutions are needed at every level of society. Indeed, why should we believe that the changes needed to cope with such an interconnected world could be achieved by confining our efforts to limit parts of a very complex system? The isolated, piecemeal attempts of the past are responsible for our present economic mess. We don't for one moment believe that our present economic difficulties would somehow magically disappear if the dollar were painlessly devalued, if the Japanese yen were revalued, if the correct fiscal policies were somehow established, or if the federal budget were balanced and the huge deficits reduced. No one, least of all us, denies that these remedies would help significantly; however, they are only *part* of the total solution.

The basic problem facing the United States today is one of organization. The traditional means by which products and services have been delivered no longer work. The solution must be matched to the nature of the problem; otherwise, as has occurred so often in the past, an inappropriate quick fix will result, perpetuating the basic problem.

Because the basic problem is organizational, we believe that examination of the current debate over the need for national institutions to steer the economy is necessary. Such examination not only introduces new issues that top-level executives, in particular, need to consider; it also reinforces and further clarifies many of the points made in previous chapters. Redesigning a national institution(s) to steer the U.S. economy is not different *in principle* from redesigning an individual firm or industry to compete in a global economy. Given the magnitude of the effort and the number of groups involved, however, reorganization at the national level is naturally much more difficult and, hence, much more problematic politically. We are nonetheless convinced that it is necessary. To argue as directly as possible, even if every manager in the United States reoriented his or her thinking along the lines of Chapter Three, or if every firm or industry reorganized along the lines of Chapters Four and Five, it would still not be enough. Action at the national level would be necessary to compete successfully in the global economy.

This chapter is divided into two parts. First, we broadly outline, in terms of the six key variables discussed in Chapter Four, the arguments for and against a national industrial policy and hence, by implication, for and against an institution(s) to *orchestrate but not control* the national economy. In brief, a national industrial policy is a series of proposals that would provide support for those industries that the government thinks can compete successfully on the world scene. As the issue has most often been posed (not always correctly, we would note), it is an institutionalized process for choosing and supporting "winning" versus "losing" industries. We conclude that not only does the United States need a national industrial policy (IP) but, as a number of analysts have noted, we already have one by fiat (Magaziner and Reich, 1983; Reich, 1985; and Thurow, 1985a). We merely add that it seems virtually impossible, by the definition of a national economy, for an IP not to have existed.

In the second part of the chapter, we discuss the considerable lessons that have been learned, largely from the Japanese, on designing an institution for forming and implementing an IP. As we show, these two aspects, forming and implementing an IP, are inseparable. You can't do one without the other.

We must, however, be very clear with regard to what we have to learn from the Japanese. We are calling for neither uncritical acceptance nor slavish imitation. We cannot adopt wholesale what the Japanese have fashioned. The Japanese have thirty years of experience in *experimentation* with institutional forms for managing an economy. The case is very much akin to General Motors's (GM's) development of the Saturn project, or better yet, experiment. As we stressed in Chapters Four and Five, the point is *not* whether Saturn *solves* GM's problems in narrowing the gap between it and Japanese carmakers in small-car production costs. The point is that GM as a corporation has committed itself to experimentation. It realizes that it must change radically to survive (although recent events challenge seriously whether GM really does realize this). Saturn is only one prototype for the factory of the future. If it fails, it proves only that it was the wrong prototype. It does not prove that the concept, a factory of the future, has failed, only that we have not yet discovered and implemented the correct one (Fisher, 1985). One experiments to learn what to do better next time, not necessarily to confirm one's initial thoughts.

The Japanese have led the way in experimentation not only at the industrial level but also at the societal level. As stressed in Chapter Five, we believe that industries that do not experiment will not survive. We also believe that societies that do not experiment will not prosper economically.

When we talk about designing a national institution to implement a national IP, we're no longer talking about the culture of a particular institution. We are talking about the culture that all Americans share. As those who have written about the pros and cons of an IP seem to recognize implicitly, certain values that we as Americans share inhibit the formation and implementation of an IP (Bluestone and Harrison, 1982; Gevirtz, 1984; Magaziner and Reich, 1983; Phillips, 1984; and Thurow, 1985a). Because of their importance, we believe that these values should be discussed explicitly instead of implicitly, and therefore, we do so in Chapter Seven.

Industrial Policy, Arguments Pro and Con: Who Needs It? Can It Work?

The arguments as to whether a national IP is required to guide the United States out of its current economic malaise can be broken down into eight categories: (1) the performance of the U.S. economy relative to other economies, (2) ideological differences regarding such concepts as a "free market," (3) the inevitable politicization of an IP, (4) the inevitable bureaucratization of an IP, (5) the track record of IPs of other countries, (6) American cultural values, (7) the preference for internal versus external role models, and (8) the scope of an IP. (For an introduction to the many issues and arguments, pro and con, for a national IP, see Bluestone and Harrison, 1982; Gevirtz, 1984; Magaziner and Reich, 1983; Phillips, 1984; Reich, 1983; Vogel, 1985.) Let us consider each category.

The first category is the easiest to assess and to counter. All the evidence indicates that since World War II, it has been increasingly difficult to single out industries in which the United States has not lost significant ground or surrendered a lead (see Scott and Lodge, 1985; and Magaziner and Reich, 1983). Not only has the United States's share of external world markets (for example, autos and steel) declined, but its internal domestic markets have been penetrated by foreign competitors. As stated in an article in *Business Week,* "Relentlessly, Japanese companies have moved into Western markets and swept aside the local suppliers. In microwave ovens, which the U.S. invented, the process took just 15 years. . . . Japan now produces three-quarters of the world's videocassette recorders, single-lens cameras, and motorcycles. It makes half the world's ships, two-fifths of its TVs, and a third of its semiconductors and cars. . . . 'If you take manufacturing, the Japanese are winning it all,' says James C. Abegglen, former head of Boston Consulting Group Inc.'s Tokyo office, who is now a professor of business at Tokyo's Sophia University" (Dobrzynski and others, 1985, p. 62).

In itself, the clear loss of leadership in world and domestic markets does not establish the need for an industrial policy for all industries. It does, however, show that fundamental structural reforms are needed at the industry level as well as at the company level. Consider as one example the textile industry. Since 1980, some 250 textile mills have closed, 48 during 1985 alone (Engardio, 1985). It is estimated that at the present pace, imports will constitute 80 percent of the U.S. market by 1990. The result may be the elimination of more than half (915,000) of the jobs in the textile industry and an additional 943,000 jobs in related industries. What's truly sad, according to Roger Milliken, president of Milliken & Company, is that the "inefficient mills have already been shaken out" (Engardio, 1985). This means that the next to go will be the efficient, improved mills. Efficiency at the company level is no longer sufficient.

When we exclude the various survival strategies available to the industry and the proposed strict tariffs and import restrictions to which the Reagan administration is opposed, the alternative which remains is fascinating. Essentially it is the elimination of fragmentation, the lack of cooperation among textile makers, apparel companies (the largest customers of the textile companies), and even retailers. As stated in *Business Week,*

Although they can't match Asia's low labor rates, apparel companies could react faster to market

changes. They are so fragmented—there are 14,000
garment makers—that they lack leverage to force
textile companies to change colors or fill small orders for hot fabrics in less than six months' time.
... [it is estimated] that better coordination between makers of textiles and apparel could cut lead
times for new products to an average of 17 weeks
and slash domestic prices by 15%.
  ... The question is how much of the industry will remain by the time it has learned [through
such devices as consolidation and coordination] to
be competitive [Engardio, 1985, p. 54].

The case of the textile industry is not an isolated one. It
has beset the mini steel mills established in the late 1970s and
early 1980s, on the basis of reversal of outdated assumptions, as
discussed in Chapter Five. It was thought that small mills incor-
porating the latest steel-making technology would be able to
compete successfully in specialty, niche markets. The trouble,
again, is that the most efficient technology and plants are still
not enough to compete in world markets. As Sheets (1985)
stated in a recent article in *U.S. News & World Report,*

Threats seem to outnumber opportunities. The
high-priced dollar is drawing more imported steel
into the country. Big Steel, aided by union wage
concessions, is becoming more competitive. And
success has bred imitations—minis waging war
against each other in an effort to maintain profits
in a glutted market.
  Most minis, though, are affected by the same
forces rocking the foundation of the entire U.S.
steel industry [p. 51].

More interesting are the ideological arguments in the second category. These arguments are akin to positions accepted
on faith. Either one believes in the continuation of the free-
market economy or one does not. Or, rather, one continues to

believe in the ideal of a free-market economy versus a managed
economy, even when departures from the ideal become so pronounced as to strain credibility.

What's particularly interesting about these arguments is
that some of the most powerful foes of a free-market economy
come from quite unexpected quarters. Thus, in *Staying on Top:
The Business Case for a National Industrial Strategy* (1984),
Kevin Phillips strongly castigates fellow conservatives for per-
sisting in the fantasy that the United States either operates, or
can continue to operate, according to the dictates of a classic
free-market economy. The fact is that we no longer have a
world economy governed by free trade, perfect competition,
absence of governmentally imposed barriers to entering foreign
markets, slowly changing world technology, and ample time for
adjustment of markets everywhere to equilibrium. What we find
is the complete opposite. *There exists no major economy that is
not significantly influenced by its government in the operation
of its industries or markets.* The intervention assumes a variety
of forms: tax breaks to fledgling industries, which protect them
until they are able to compete against established players; low-
cost government-financed loans, which provide cheap capital
and, hence, allow firms to compete on favorable grounds on the
world scene; low-cost loans and tax credits for research and development. Therefore, it's no use for Americans to complain
that foreign governments and companies are not playing by the
established rules of the economic game. They are not playing by
the old rules because they have deliberately set out to change
the rules to their advantage. The United States can either get
everyone to shift back to the old rules (which is no longer feasible), learn to play by the new rules (which is possible), or, what
is our position, evolve a set of rules that will force the game to a
higher level for all parties. To achieve this last option, however,
it is necessary to understand the new rules, and that can only be
done by using them for a considerable time.

With the third category, the arguments begin to get really
interesting. Here the main argument against an IP is its inevitable politicization, given both the nature of special-interest
groups in this country, with their single-issue focus, and the

natural instinct of Washington politicians to cater to these interests. Hence, the formation and execution of an IP would inevitably reach a stalemate between those who want support given
to old, dying industries like steel, and the workers who have
been displaced from them, and those who want support given to
fledgling, high-technology industries upon which the nation's
future industrial base appears to rest.

There is another side: we already have an IP by fiat; it's
already politicized; it couldn't help but be; therefore, what's
really new about politicization? Hence, instead of having a haphazard IP that has emerged by fiat, it's better to bring it out in
the open and debate it for all to see and to participate in it
more fully (Magaziner and Reich, 1983; Scott and Lodge, 1985).

The argument that we already have an IP by fiat rests on
the fact that the U.S. government has heavily supported a host
of industries, such as agriculture, aircraft, auto, housing, steel,
and transportation, and that without such support these industries would not have enjoyed the success they once had. Further, to pretend that the vast array of import quotas, tariffs,
and voluntary export agreements are somehow exceptions is de-
lusive. To pretend that we do not have a national IP is to ignore
conveniently that "the federal government is the largest single
consumer of goods and services in the United States" (Magaziner and Reich, 1983). In 1979, for instance, the government
awarded over $94 billion in contracts through a host of various
federal agencies. "About 75 percent of the total was spent by
the Department of Defense, another 4 percent by the National
Aeronautics and Space Administration for the U.S. space program, 6 percent by the Department of Energy" (Magaziner and
Reich, 1983).

Additional facts are no less staggering and damaging to
the pernicious notion that a nation of the size and complexity
of the United States could run without an IP of some kind. For
instance:

> About 50 percent of the research and development
> undertaken in the U.S. is funded by the federal
> government. . . . While the overwhelming bulk of

this effort is related to defense, government R&D funding is critical to many industries. For example, in 1977, [the] government provided 70 percent of the development funding for the aircraft industry and 48 percent for the communication equipment industry. During the same year, the government funded only 1 percent of R&D in the pharmaceuticals industry. . . . While such differentials no doubt affect military needs, they also have an important bearing on the relative commercial development of these industries [Magaziner and Reich, 1983, p. 278].

In a similar vein,

Unfortunately, none of [the numerous industry support] programs has been viewed through the lens of international competitiveness nor have any been seen as an aspect of a coherent industrial policy. Instead, each program has been formulated by the agencies and congressional subcommittees that are closest to well-established industries and are therefore most susceptible to special pleading. The result is a political hodgepodge of subsidies. . . . The government now spends five times more money on R&D for commercial fisheries than on R&D for steel; $455 million in tax breaks for the timber industry, but none for the semiconductor industry; over $6 billion in loans and loan guarantees to the shipbuilding industry and $940 million in loans to the auto industry [Magaziner and Reich, 1983, pp. 241-242].

Thus, who's kidding whom about the sudden appearance of politicization? It couldn't help but be there all the time in a society as complex as ours (Navaro, 1984). If an IP has merit, its implementation ought not to be decided on the basis of politicization. Instead, it ought to be decided on the basis of whether institutions can be redesigned so that the inevitable politicization to which they will always be subject can be handled in ways that are most beneficial to our nation's economic health.

The fourth category concerns the bureaucratization that would inevitably accompany the operation of any agency concerned with forming and implementing an IP. Why, critics ask (Badaracco and Yoffie, 1983; Gevirtz, 1984; Kantrow, 1983), should we believe that a group of Washington-based bureaucrats acting far from where new businesses are developed could do a better job of picking potential winning industries than those who develop them? Further, the critics contend, the information requirements necessary to make intelligent choices are overwhelming. For these and other, related reasons, it is highly doubtful that anyone or any highly centralized agency could make the choices for a society as complex as the United States than the free, unfettered, operation of the open market. On the surface, at least, these challenges are formidable and not lightly dismissed. They are serious enough that they deserve more extensive treatment than this section can provide and, therefore, are discussed at greater length in the next section. Suffice it to say that the information and personnel requirements necessary to form and implement an IP are formidable but not impossible. The critics are right in the sense that an IP will not work with either ordinary information or typical bureaucrats. However, they are wrong in the sense that we can specify the people, job, and information requirements for an IP. They are also wrong in assuming that because these requirements are severe, the job of designing an institution to form and implement an IP is hopeless and impossible. Nonetheless, we would do well to heed the critics because any design that does not meet their criticisms will not work.

In the fifth category, which is closely related to the fourth category, the basic argument is that because the track record of other nations is hardly perfect, whether we could do any better is questionable. For instance, the case of Honda is widely touted by the critics. As is known, the Japanese did not target the Honda Motor Car Company for special attention. As a result,

Honda was forced to act on its own without government special support. The response to these charges is that no one contends that any institution will ever be perfect in picking or assisting potential winners. Likewise, no one contends that the IPs of all countries, and the institutions for their implementation, are equal. Admittedly, some are better than others. But, most important of all, the IPs of the Japanese have, on the whole, proved superior to those of the Europeans. As a result, the Japanese provide clearer lessons.

In many ways, this category of arguments shoves us back to the first. The policies and institutions of no nation are perfect and hence free from substantial criticism; however, it does not follow that nations following different rules cannot do better than those who have not learned to adapt to new conditions. Again, the data overwhelmingly demonstrate that those nations that play by different rules, of which an IP is an important component, are besting us at a game in which we were once the undisputed winner.

As is natural, the different categories intertwine and hence are somewhat repetitious. This is true of the arguments in the sixth category. Americans are a fiercely independent people, so this argument goes, with a character shaped by the traditions of Jefferson. As a result, individualism is indelibly stamped on our character. As a people we are unwilling to let others, no matter how competent, make decisions for us that we feel we can make better. The basic traditions and values of small-town America, unlike the institutions of the Japanese, work against the establishment of an IP here (Phillips, 1984).

These arguments are also formidable and not easily dismissed. We take them so seriously that we have devoted an entire chapter (Chapter Seven) to examination of those aspects of our national character that need to change, and the prospects for accomplishing such change, to implement an effective IP in the United States. The outcome of this examination is that although the task is not impossible, it is extremely difficult. Indeed, some values are so imbedded in the American character that they appear incapable of being changed significantly. This is all the more paradoxical because the United States today does not at all resemble nineteenth-century small-town America. Today the United States is a large, complex, highly interdependent, organized America governed by overlapping and interacting institutions whose purview extends to every nook and cranny of our lives. If anything, we are becoming more complex and organized, not less. And yet, perhaps because of this very trend, we cling to the myth of a simple America. As a result, our underlying values are dangerously out of sync with today's world. This means that the more an IP is needed, the harder it is to achieve. We must be very careful here because the stakes are so big. In the spirit of Chapter Three, we must be careful to distinguish between an *absolutely binding, unchangeable constraint* and a *current, changeable obstacle*. The assessment as to which we face cannot be made on the basis of a superficial analysis of our national character.

The seventh category of arguments questions (Gevirtz, 1984) the need to emulate foreign models for development when, presumably, the best ones available are here at home. According to Gevirtz (1984),

> Armed with only a small amount of capital, with the weight of government regulation and taxation against them, America's entrepreneurs over the past decade have produced virtually all the nation's new private sector jobs and the bulk of its innovations while increasingly earning far higher returns on equity [p. 15].

> Between 1969 and 1976 small firms with less than twenty employees created as many as two-thirds of all the nation's new jobs. . . . In marked contrast, the Fortune 500 firms, after doubling their numbers of jobs between 1954 and 1970, failed to generate any new jobs and actually began reducing their payrolls. As the 1980s began, this trend intensified with over 1.3 million workers laid off by giant firms that reduced work forces to levels below those of ten years earlier [p. 17].

And thus,

> Obsessed with foreign models, Vogel and others of
> like mind largely ignore the creative role of entre-
> preneurs in the revival of America's industrial
> greatness. Robert Reich, for instance, hails the con-
> fluence of giant institutions in France, Japan, and
> West Germany for helping "enhance the creation
> of wealth." Comparing the performance of Ameri-
> can and foreign steelmakers, Reich praises govern-
> ment-backed programs abroad that assist the com-
> petitiveness of major industrial firms and he suggests
> America adopt a similar industrial policy. Instead
> of the traditional ethos of individualism, he de-
> scribes major corporations as the designated
> "agents of society" who must work in close con-
> junction with elite bureaucrats to determine na-
> tional economic policies.
>   Fixated on the failures of America's giants,
> Reich and other advocates of foreign-style govern-
> ment intervention seem utterly oblivious to the
> massive entrepreneurial transformation of the last
> decade [pp. 143-144].

As proponents of an IP, we don't agree with Gevirtz. The
fundamental argument is not whether the role of the entrepreneur can be ignored. No one denies that America owes its tremendous economic success to the creative genius and risk-taking
abilities of its people. The question is whether this *alone* is
enough in a world in which we compete against foreign firms
that are backed by the resources of their governments. Granted
that entrepreneurs have been and will continue to be one of the
most, if not the most, potent forces for change in our society.
But what makes them exempt from all the forces we've been
discussing? Are we to survive as a society of perpetual small
start-ups? Granted also that there may be an inherent upper limit to the size of firms, that beyond a certain size organizations
become trapped in their own structures, which turn against

them and defeat their effectiveness (Ginzberg and Vojta, 1985). None of this mitigates the fact that somewhere we need institutions of size to serve, if only to coordinate, the interests of societies of the magnitude of a United States. One does not avoid large problems by restricting the size of individual firms. One merely shifts the problem to other institutions that must coordinate it for a complex society. This is not to say that we do not need the continual infusion of new ideas and products from small firms that are not inhibited by the tired constraints and assumptions of dinosaur firms and industries. Rather, it is extremely difficult to envision that we will not need some institutions of scale to cope with the problems of today's world. Even if they are small in size, they must be big in scope to comprehend the environment. Again, we find a refusal to acknowledge the realities of today's world in this harkening back to a simpler, if not idealized, world that no longer exists, if indeed it ever did.

It would be even easier to accept the arguments against IPs at the federal level if IPs were not already operating at the state and city levels. Why not at all levels? As reported in a recent article in *Fortune,*

> In no fewer than 27 [states], a special advisory body appointed by the governor has recommended programs of some sort to promote research and development, improve education and training, and facilitate industrial growth. More often than not, the suggestions have called for an expanded role by the government.
>
> . . . Some states [even] take equity positions in start-up companies. What's behind all this is concern that the unaided free market will not create enough new jobs.
>
> States are also forging new links between universities and private industry, creating "research incubators" . . . —places for hatching new products and services. The states give budding entrepreneurs low-rent office space, usually near a campus, where

they can use a university's research labs and perhaps tap into its computer.

... Michigan, for example, has created the Industrial Technology Institute to work on robotics and other aspects of the factory of the future. The state kicked in $17.5 million [Bernstein, 1984].

In the same vein,

In 1982, Michigan passed a law allowing up to 5% of its public-employee pension funds to be used as venture capital. Suddenly the state was one of the nation's biggest venture-capital firms with $450 million under management, and Michigan became the leader among states in direct investment in emerging technology-based companies. ... It has invested $33 million in 21 firms [Woutat, 1984].

At the city level, there is the example of Spartanburg, South Carolina. Over the past five years, the town lost 3000 jobs in the textile industry. Seeing the handwriting on the wall and "not willing to wait for someone else to save them" (Treadwell, 1985, p. 13), the town decided to take matters into its own hands. It therefore decided to seek foreign investors long before the state made the decision to do so. In the beginning, the plan was to bring in foreign businesses that could serve the area's textile industry. However, long-term plans include attracting $770 million in new investments by 1988 to create 8000 new jobs. The industries sought by the town range from printing and publishing to robotics, automation, banking, and equipment leasing. As a vice-president of one of the largest textile mills in town puts it, "We're just very fortunate that we're not one of the little towns where the mill is all that they had and now it's gone" (Treadwell, 1985, p. 13). Spartanburg is fortunate because it no longer believes the myth of completely free markets. As a result, it is not constrained from managing its own destiny by entering into a partnership with local industry, that is, its own mini IP.

Finally, there are signs of a new form of organization—
the international institution. In a recent article in the *Los Angeles Times,* Henry Kissinger called for Japan and the United
States to take the lead in generously supporting new institutions: "Japan could serve both the world and its national interest by generously supporting multilateral institutions devoted to
global economic growth. In establishing the limit of an acceptable trade imbalance, the United States should give heavy
weight to a Japanese contribution to global economic growth
substantially exceeding its current efforts" (1984, p. 2). As
Utopian as such proposals seem, they are not that far-fetched.
We are closer than ever to the concept of *world firms.* In contrast to multinationals, which are owned by one firm and have
their home base in one country, the world firm will be what its
name implies. It will be jointly owned and managed *by both the
firms and the governments* of more than one country. One can
see the roots of this development in today's events; an example
is a recent experience at GM:

> In 1972, GM entered a 50-50 joint venture with
> South Korea's Chinjin group, a conglomerate with
> diverse interests outside the automotive field. The
> joint company was to make automotive parts and,
> eventually, cars and trucks.
>
> Three years later, the Chinjin group became
> overextended. . . . To secure a loan from the Kore-
> an Development Bank, it pledged its shares in the
> GM joint venture. Then it defaulted.
>
> "Suddenly, we found ourselves partners with
> the Korean government, which owned the bank,"
> said Barton Brown, GM's [vice-president] for
> Asian and African operations. "Actually, it wasn't
> a bad relationship, but it wasn't the bank's bag and
> they got our approval to turn over their shares to
> Daewoo," South Korea's second largest business
> group. Despite some early rough patches, the GM-
> Daewoo relationship continues today [Gibson,
> 1985, p. 5].

Finally, we come to the last (eighth) set of arguments, which concern the scope, or aspirations, of an IP. Firmly opposed to an industrial *policy* (IP), Phillips (1984) is nonetheless a staunch proponent of an industrial *strategy* (IS). The difference is not one of semantics. Phillips readily admits that we are far from the world of a free market that can be understood independently of new institutions at the national level. He also clearly understands that other nations are playing by rules into which IPs have deliberately been built. Thus he clearly recognizes that we need new institutions at the national level, even representation in the Cabinet, to gather and coordinate information. Phillips stops just short of having such institutions pick winners versus losers on the basis of such information.

The basic question, of course, is if an agency is good and trusted enough to gather, digest, and disseminate the "appropriate information" to guide the informed choices of others, why isn't it good and trusted enough to make the final choice? Can it really do one without the other? This does not mean that it would exercise an autocratic role, for in fact that is not what occurs in the best foreign IP models. There is significant participation by a multitude of parties in the formation of an IP.

The whole argument in this last category is reminiscent of one offered by Kissinger (1969) in a very important and well-received book, *Nuclear Weapons and Foreign Policy*. Kissinger realized early that all-out nuclear war was sheer madness and hence completely out of the question because no one would win such a war. Hence, talking about the possibility of nuclear war, let alone planning for it, was not sensible. He was convinced that the United States, and hopefully the Soviet Union, had to think seriously about the possibility of limited nuclear wars because nuclear weapons were clearly not going to vanish. Thus, nuclear weapons have changed the rules of war just as the new competition has changed the rules of global economics. Kissinger thus strongly advocated that we formulate policies for fighting wars based on the limited use of nuclear weapons. However, he realized that to limit a nuclear war, both sides would have to show great trust and cooperation. If they could not, then in the heat of battle, it would be very easy to misread the enemy's signals and hence escalate to an all-out nuclear war. It is strange indeed that having obtained this level of insight regarding nuclear policy, Kissinger did not take the next step and reach the inevitable conclusion of his argument. Namely, if the two parties were able to trust one another and cooperate in limiting a nuclear war, then why go to war in the first place? And if such trust and cooperation did not exist in the first place, why would such qualities appear in the heat of battle? Some twenty-eight years have passed since Kissinger wrote his book; no one has answered these vital questions yet.

The parallel with our principal question should be clear. If an agency of impeccable trust and competency is required to form and implement an IP, then why can't it take the next step and help to choose those industries that should be given support?

We conclude that the arguments do not overwhelmingly support or refute the need for an IP and for an institution to formulate and implement it. The critics are right in their contention that major obstacles would have to be overcome to institute an IP in the United States. Nonetheless, we remain convinced of the need, basically because *the successful design and implementation of an IP pose no more, no fewer problems than are already present.* What its critics fail to realize is that if we can't design and implement an IP then we really can't respond successfully to the challenges of the global economy.

Critical Design Factors in an American "Ministry of International Trade and Industry"

The Japanese governmental institution known as the Ministry of International Trade and Industry (MITI) is undoubtedly the most successful role model and one that we would be wise to scrutinize. Over thirty years of experience with this and other institutions have taught the Japanese how to design mechanisms for competing in world markets. The whole experience of the Japanese is a pointed example of the phenomenon "less is more" (see Chapter Eight). Devastated by World War II, their industry and country in ruins, and lacking huge internal markets and the necessary capital and the infrastructure to supply their people, the Japanese were forced to seek out and cultivate outside markets to rebuild their country and their economy. In retrospect, a humiliating military defeat, from which, some commentators note, the Japanese have still not recovered psychologically, became the seed of an enormous economic victory (Stokes, 1985).

Through their experience, the Japanese have discovered key principles that match the six variables inherent in the design of all organizations. We briefly discuss five of these variables here and reserve treatment of the most important one, national culture, for the next chapter.

First, the institutional structure of MITI is as straightforward as possible. For instance, the Tokyo office of MITI has only around 2500 officials; the entire ministry, only 12,000 (Jameson and Redburn, 1983). Its aim from the very beginning was formation of one agency with authority over all affairs pertaining to Japanese industry (Magaziner and Reich, 1983). Contrast this with the United States. Despite high-level White House councils that are supposed to coordinate U.S. economic policy, it remains highly fragmented, almost intentionally, it would seem, by design. Programs to promote and regulate international trade, foreign economic policy, foreign investment, and related research and development are controlled by almost every branch, agency, and committee of the U.S. government (Magaziner and Reich, 1983)! Little wonder why Phillips noted that "because our trade policy is so decentralized, foreign lobbyists can literally shop around to get the best deal they want" (1984, p. 89). They exploit the advantages that accrue from our bureaucratic fragmentation. This underlines the necessity of establishing an institution to develop and manage an IP. If we can't design a more effective central organization for forming national economic policy, then we can't manage it at all.

Carefully note that in line with the variables discussed in Chapter Four, the Japanese have designed a structure that deliberately promotes *integration* of related functions. In other words, they have not left to chance the coordination of vital activities at the national level. To visualize the strategy involved in designing an organization with a global integrated view of the economy, consider the departments of MITI. The basic unit is the sector, or what is called an industry in the United States. As Vogel notes, "the various sections of MITI are responsible for corresponding sectors of industry and commerce, but the interests of these sectors are balanced at the highest levels in the ministry and officials rotate among sections so as always to keep in mind MITI's overall mission" (Vogel, 1985, p. 64). If an organization with a global view of the economy is desired, then it must be deliberately designed for that purpose. It's not impossible that such a purpose can be realized by happenstance, but we wouldn't bet on it with so much at stake.

Second, what of the people who inhabit such an organization? Here the critics of a U.S. IP are right but for the wrong reasons. Partly from their experience and partly because of their historical traditions and different relationships to government, the Japanese have found that you cannot run a MITI that has to deal with many important sectors of society and inspire trust and respect without an elite core of personnel. As a result, the top technical graduates from the top universities are recruited annually for key positions. By "technical" is meant the engineering and economic professions, thus ensuring MITI the expertise it needs to make the best informed analyses and recommendations humanly possible. As stated in an article in the *Los Angeles Times,* "Every year, 25 engineering graduates and 25 law and economic specialists enter the ranks of MITI top-echelon bureaucrats—an elite from which MITI will choose its section chiefs, bureau chiefs, and, ultimately, one vice minister, to run the 12,000-person ministry. With careers normally lasting 30 years, MITI is staffed at the top by about 1,500 of those cream-of-the-crop leaders. This year [1983], 1,370 of Japan's top college graduates competed for the 50 posts, which gave the ministry the ability to skim even more selectively from Japan's brightest students" (Jameson and Redburn, 1983, p. 3).

Third, of all the variables, the tasks, or how MITI actually works, may be the most fascinating and important. MITI officials do *not* have the power to command and give loans directly to promising companies within an industry that is targeted for development. Instead, they must persuade others, the Development Bank and the Export-Import Bank, to accept their recommendations, all of which are arrived at after careful study and consultation with numerous stakeholders in Japanese society. Furthermore, the system works only *after* the so-called free-market system has completed its initial phase. That is, once an industry has been targeted for special attention, all-out, unaided competition is allowed to develop between private firms within that industry. Only after it becomes clear who the top five or so winners of this competition are, that is, those companies that are achieving significant economies of scale in manufacturing new products, does MITI step in. These companies are then given special help in the form of low-cost loans, subsidies, tax breaks, and so on, to help them establish a niche in world markets. In addition, these companies are allowed to consult and choose those parts of the market on which each will concentrate. Thus they are not restrained from sharing information by antitrust laws as are U.S. companies. What's amazing is that Japanese companies have learned how to share important information without giving away vital secrets.

Vogel (1985) provides a good summary of the picture thus far: "MITI officials have power to grant licenses and patents to determine which firms will participate in which projects, but the real power of MITI rests on the quality of its information, the care it takes in consulting with outsiders, the persuasiveness of its arguments, and the will to use its persuasiveness to favor those firms that cooperate. MITI officials have not always proved correct in their projections, but their thoroughness and the close consultation with business spreads the burden of error, and like private business leaders they can change their estimates as new information becomes available" (p. 64).

What then is the special quality of this information, the fourth key variable? The distinctive quality of the information is that it enables MITI to see and to present the big picture of worldwide competition. Again and again, this key lesson emerges: *The big picture will rarely make it through a system that has not been deliberately designed to allow its emergence.* Thus, MITI officials may not do the actual research, but they collect information, keep informed, and, in some cases, institute projects that allow them to see the big picture. Although we are not sure, we suspect that to achieve this goal they must be doing something akin to monitoring high-level, critical assumptions for whole industries as we attempted to do in Chapter Five. Even if they are not, this would certainly be one of our main recommendations regarding the key functions of a MITI-like organization with Cabinet-level status in the U.S. government.

Finally, what about the reward system that drives MITI? The nature of the rewards is rooted in Japanese culture and thus poses, once again, the challenge of whether our culture has the values necessary to develop a MITI-like organization suited to our experience. Vogel (1985) has put it well: "Since the late nineteenth century, Japanese society has measured success of bureaucrats concerned with various sectors of the economy by the achievements of their sector. This accountability provided the personal drive for bureaucrats that sustained a tradition of governmental assistance to industry. Beginning at the same time, American society measured the success of comparable bureaucrats not by achievements of the sector under them but by how well they enforced the rules, and this sustained a tradition of adversarial relations and control over industry. The Japanese bureaucrat responsible for the success of his sector has a powerful incentive to help his team do well against rivals, foreign or domestic" (p. 166).

The notion that the world will get by with fewer institutions is naive. That we need new institutions that are more effective is a proposition with which we are in strong agreement. And for such institutions to be effective requires that they not be bureaucratic in the traditional sense. We are as skeptical as any of the critics of IP that such institutions will actually be established. But we cannot let such skepticism lead to hopeless despair or to our ceasing to argue in favor of an IP or to participate in the design of new institutions. Fundamentally, we believe not only that such institutions are inevitable but that they will multiply and evolve despite our extreme individualism. The time is ripe.

With respect to the host of proposals that have been, and are being, put forward by others, we are in strong agreement. For instance, we agree with the need for nationwide job retraining programs for displaced workers (Bluestone and Harrison, 1982). That we do not have such programs in the numbers required is a national disgrace (Vogel, 1985). Surely the workers are not entirely to blame for the condition of their outmoded industries. We also agree with Gevirtz (1984) when he argues that breaks in the form of tax credits ought not to go only to large, established corporations. Small, fledgling start-ups deserve such breaks for investment in research and development no less than their larger, more established counterparts.

On one thing above all we are highly insistent. *No support of any kind ought to be given to any organization, large or small, old or new, high or low technology, that is not willing to make such support contingent on well-thought-out plans for substantial innovation.* No organization ought to be rewarded for perpetuating the conditions that brought it to the state where it needs support.

We view the 200 or so bills currently before the U.S. Congress calling for the protectionist support of this or that beleaguered industry as just one more symptom of the fragmentation that haunts our entire society. How well can 200 of anything fare against foreign competitors who see coordination as the way to compete?

We should exercise a word of caution. Because we have much to learn from the experience of others such as the Japanese does not mean that we are oblivious to the substantial criticisms that have surfaced recently regarding some aspects of these cultures (Sethi, Nobuaki, and Swanson, 1984). Surely the desire to learn the values of others is not a wholesale endorsement of these values. But learn and change we must, no matter from which quarter of the globe our lessons come.

Finally, in closing, we present one last example that not only bears on IP but presents a powerful case favoring a national IP.

One of the newest industries in which we seek a competitive advantage is space, specifically, the manufacture of machine parts and pharmaceutical drugs that are difficult to produce under Earth-based gravity conditions. For instance, it is much easier to produce round spheres (for example, ball bearings) under the zero-gravity conditions in space than it is here on Earth.

The potential business is estimated to be between $100 and $200 billion by the year 2000. To get an idea of what this represents, the aviation industry—one of our largest and most successful industries—is currently a $100 billion business (Osborne, 1985).

The problem is the same one we've encountered repeatedly:

> Foreign companies, particularly in France, Germany, [and Japan] have expressed a willingness to invest now for profits that they may not see for fifteen or twenty years—a luxury that very few American companies can afford.
>
> ... Given the short-term focus of most American corporations and financial institutions, the American economy depends to a great extent on entrepreneurs to provide the technological breakthroughs important to growth. So much capital is usually needed to work in space, however, that few garage entrepreneurs have a chance.
>
> Even aerospace companies, which have the expertise to create new industries in space, are not expected to take the initiative. . . . Having generated guaranteed profits for their stockholders for years on government contracts aerospace executives are unlikely to roll the dice a new product or service whose market is *not* guaranteed.
>
> In France, Germany, and Japan, the government develops strategies for the commercial exploitation of space and then works hand-in-hand with business to bring them to fruition—a textbook example of "industrial policy" [Osborne, 1985, p. 53].

The irony is that even though the current administration is opposed to an IP, it has one by fiat with respect to space. It does this by subsidizing the space shuttle to the tune of $175,000,000 per mission to the benefit of communications satellite companies. But, if it can subsidize these companies, why not others? Why not just admit once and for all that we not only have, but have always had, IPs, that we can't get by without them?

We return to Vogel's questions at the beginning of this chapter; only now there's a new twist. The question no longer is How many old-line industries will we have to lose before we realize we cannot save our economy through such outmoded notions as the free market? Rather, the question is How many new, fledgling businesses will we have to lose before we realize we cannot play a fundamentally new game by outmoded rules?

7

An American National Industrial Policy: A Cultural and Political Oxymoron?

"A Japanese banker and a member of Japan's Ministry of International Trade & Industry had a quiet talk recently. The man from MITI was trying to persuade the banker to grant a loan for a long-range industrial development. The bank was balking. The MITI man asked the banker: 'Do you expect your bank to be around longer than Japan?' End of argument.

"This illustrates a familiar point: The Japanese are fiercely competitive, but cooperation takes precedence when the issue is national economic survival. Americans are no strangers to the idea of national purpose, especially in wartime. Where they differ from the Japanese is that national unity and long-range thinking do not extend to the economic front" (Jonas, 1986, p. 84).

Executive Summary

Old Organizing Assumptions	*New Organizing Assumptions*
1. The basic, traditional values that made the United States great are still sufficient to make it great today.	1. The basic, traditional values do not need to be abandoned in their entirety but they must be seriously adapted and modi-

Old Organizing Assumptions	New Organizing Assumptions
	fied if the United States is to be competitive.
2. Rampant individualism is still the best way for the United States to compete.	2. Individualism must be tempered by serious teamwork if the United States is to be competitive.
3. The most serious threats facing the United States today are external; they were well anticipated by George Orwell in his view of totalitarian societies.	3. The most serious threats today are internal; they were well anticipated by Aldous Huxley in his view of the extreme debilitating effects that unrestrained pursuit of pleasure would have on society's ability to cope with complexity.

It has become highly fashionable in recent years to discuss organizational culture, that is, a set of unwritten, barely articulated values, beliefs, and assumptions that, because they are largely unconscious, exert a profound influence on the behavior of an organization. Fashionable or not, the subject is legitimate because culture is to an organization what personality is to an individual (Kilmann, 1984; Kilmann, Saxton, Serpa, and Associates, 1985; Schein, 1985). Culture thus allows one to get to the deeper issues that influence a corporation as strongly as any of its so-called rational or readily observable surface features. Unfortunately, it has not yet become fashionable to discuss, in a comparable manner, the bearing of national culture on policies that affect all organizations in America. This is our purpose in this chapter.

If there is one value that is the key to understanding American culture, surely that value is individualism. Individualism is so central that the distinguished Berkeley sociologist Robert N. Bellah and his colleagues (1985) have devoted an entire book to it: *Habits of the Heart: Individualism and Commitment in American Life* is a skillful study of the values that Americans hold dear today. It was written on the basis of hundreds of interviews of Americans from all walks of life conducted over a five-year period. Bellah and his colleagues conclude that individualism lies at the very core of American culture. The belief that the individual is the ultimate, indivisible unit of reality, existence, and freedom is so dear to Americans that it permeates all their thoughts and actions. For most Americans, individualism has a special meaning, the right to be "left alone" by anyone or anything that would restrict thought or action. In this form, it has a negative connotation: *freedom from* the influence and control of others. As a result, few Americans have any well-thought-out ideas or systematic plans regarding the use of this freedom to accomplish positive goals.

More often, individualism in our society is linked with economic freedom and the operation of a free market in which clear-cut measures of performance determine the winners and losers. As a consequence, many Americans find it very hard, if not impossible, to join with others. An understanding of the reasons is vital. If individualism finds its ultimate vindication in the fact that it can be measured "objectively" as individual economic success, then collective action, or community, fares far less well. Religion, marriage, family, and community, all of which have served to form the collective bonds among us, are increasingly relegated to spheres of "subjective" action. In none of these spheres do we find a concrete language for measuring success anywhere near what we supposedly enjoy in the sphere of economic individualism. Guess which spheres tend to suffer as a result? And the situation seems to have gotten worse. Bellah and his colleagues make clear that the institutions that are supposed to promote links among us have themselves become subject to the pressures of extreme individualism. For instance, consider the institution of marriage. Apparently, more and more of us believe that when a marriage no longer serves their needs and wants, the two individuals are almost obligated to walk away from it, which is apparently occurring in record numbers. Our point is not that couples should remain in an unfulfilling marriage. Rather, it is that as a culture, we failed to develop as rich a language for discussing and promoting the social good and the social collective as we have for discussing and promoting individual rights and feelings.

Bellah and his colleagues work in the tradition of the distinguished Frenchman Alexis de Tocqueville, who visited America in the nineteenth century and made the most pertinent observations of the American character yet recorded. The title of their book, *Habits of the Heart,* derives from a phrase Tocqueville ([1835, 1840] 1945) used to connote what we today would call "general culture." For Tocqueville, culture was so deep that it was literally "a habit of the heart," not just an intellectual belief that could be abandoned as easily as a style of clothing.

One of Tocqueville's brilliant observations, perhaps his most brilliant, was his clear recognition of the potential paradox contained in individualism. The extreme preoccupation of Americans with individualism could, more than anything else, potentially undermine the very conditions of their democratic freedom. If each citizen pursued and guarded individual freedom to the extreme, what force beyond the individual would look out for and serve the common good? The organizations that accomplished these greater social ends in the nineteenth century, the community meetings of small-town America, the church, and the family, are no longer strong.

At a time when more Americans nostalgically view small town America as the solution to all our problems, its existence becomes less plausible. American society is more organized and more complex than ever before. At a time when more Americans should learn to understand and to speak the language of complexity, how all things affect one another, they instead retreat deeper into a simple-minded comprehension and treatment of complex events, fragmentation, and the trivialization of all important issues (Corwin, 1983).

Like Bellah and his colleagues, we do not oppose all forms of individualism per se. We oppose only those that in the extreme cut us off from each other and prevent effective collective action. Indeed, one could argue that as a nation the United States is not individualistic enough. If individuals were secure enough of their identity independent of the masses, they wouldn't be so afraid of the need to link with others. Perhaps there would also be less materialism—people would be less likely to seek identity in material goods than in ideas and other people.

One of the most pertinent, and thereby most chilling, observations made by Bellah and his colleagues is that when individuals retreat from collective responsibility, they leave behind a social vacuum that will be filled by others who are less motivated by the common social good than by their own personal gain. Thus, extreme individualism does not eliminate the need for social institutions to manage a complex society. It only transfers that need to others who manage it less visibly and for their own gain. As stated by Bellah and colleagues (1985),

> The ambiguity and ambivalence of American individualism derive from both cultural and social contradictions. We insist, perhaps more than ever before, on finding our true selves independent of any cultural or social influence, being responsible to that self alone, and making its fulfillment the very meaning of our lives. Yet we spend much of our time navigating through immense bureaucratic structures—multiversities, corporations, government agencies—manipulating and being manipulated by others. In describing this situation, Alasdair MacIntyre has spoken of "bureaucratic individualism," the form of life exemplified by the manager and the therapist. In bureaucratic individualism, the ambiguities and contradictions of individualism are frighteningly revealed, as *freedom to make private decisions is bought at the cost of turning over most public decisions to bureaucratic managers and experts* [emphasis ours]. A bureaucratic individualism in which the consent of the governed, the first demand of modern enlightened individualism, has been abandoned in all but form, illustrates the tendency of individualism to destroy its own conditions [p. 149].

A single illustration suffices to show how profound are the effects of cultural differences on business. It certainly is sufficient to show that different cultures have very different interpretations of individualism.

The vast majority of Americans believe that Japanese culture suppresses individual identity. Thus Japanese culture is wrongly portrayed as mindless "groupism." In fact, the Japanese are individualists, but within a context entirely different from that recognized in the West (Maruyama, 1984, 1985). The Japanese view individuals within a broad cultural sense as parts of a larger pattern. As we have seen, Americans view individuals as independent of any larger pattern.

Americans also operate within a hierarchical conception of society and reality. That is, in principle, all thought and actions can be arrayed logically and abstractly within some hierarchy of concepts. Supposedly, once this hierarchy is understood, it is applicable to all situations, much as a formula is. Compare this view with that of the Japanese, who apparently do not believe that there is a universal set of principles that can be used to manage every business in every situation or culture. As a result, the Japanese are much more flexible than Americans in adapting their business practices to different situations around the world. Because they also have, or have strived to produce, a bigger picture of the world, they have also been much more aggressive in developing a presence in the world economy. This has paid off handsomely as the Japanese have gained world market leadership in several key industries, from autos to computers to electronics.

The differences in culture also help to explain key differences between American and Japanese trading practices. Because of their cultural emphasis on hierarchy, logical structure, and universal principles, Americans believe that there *ought to be* (almost in the moral sense) a *common set of rules* that *all* countries in the global economic arena obey. Thus, if Americans believe in limited trade barriers, then so should the Japanese. But the Japanese do not, because it would not give them the enormous trade advantage they now enjoy, and because it is not in line with their deep beliefs in flexibility and adaptability within the bigger picture. Thus, it would do little good for Americans to argue or wage economic war with the Japanese unless they were certain they could decisively "win" in a way that would not lead to the collapse of both economies.

What is true of the Japanese is also true of all of the major countries on the Pacific Rim: we must have a deeper understanding of their national cultures and temperaments if both they and we are to prosper economically. This understanding is necessary for smooth business operation at the individual, company, and national levels.

The Culture of Television and Television as Culture

However strong individualism is in contemporary America, it is not the only powerful cultural force propelling our society. Neil Postman (1985) makes the exceedingly strong case that the medium of television (TV) is one of the strongest forces shaping contemporary American society. It may in fact be *the* strongest shaping force:

> Television is our culture's principal mode of knowing about itself. Therefore—and this is the critical point—how television stages the world becomes the model for how the world is properly to be staged. It is not merely that on the television screen entertainment is the metaphor for all discourse. It is that off the screen the same metaphor prevails. As typography [books or discursive writing and speaking] once dictated the style of conducting politics, religion, business, education, law and other important social matters, television now takes command. In courtrooms, classrooms, operating rooms, board rooms, churches and even airplanes, Americans no longer talk to each other, they entertain each other. They do not exchange ideas; they exchange images. They do not argue with propositions; they argue with good looks, celebrities and commercials. For the message of television as metaphor is not only that all the world is a stage but that the stage is located in Las Vegas, Nevada [pp. 92-93].
>
> The result of all this is that Americans are the best entertained and quite likely the least well-informed people in the Western world [p. 106].

In a nutshell, Postman's thesis is that the United States is organized to fight the wrong enemy. In line with George Orwell's predictions, we have taken our principal enemy as the enemy from without, specifically the Soviet Union, and, accordingly, we have organized our defense establishment to meet this threat. Postman contends that we have ignored a much more powerful threat, which operates from within and which, precisely because it is hidden, actually threatens more harm.

According to Postman, it is not Orwell but Huxley to whom we should have listened. In Huxley's view, the danger was not that we would be subdued by an external foreign power. Americans are too combative to be easily overtaken by a foreign power, no matter how menacing. Huxley feared much more that we would be narcotized by an overdose of trivia, that is, junk food for the mind. No matter that Huxley predicted that drugs, instead of TV, would be the opiate of the masses. What's critical is that he made the right general prediction: the United States would be overcome by its insatiable lust for pleasure and trivia, not by an external force.

What's important is not just that TV trivializes the discussion of all important matters, but that it does so in ways that affect the entire culture:

> The fundamental assumption of [the] world [of TV] is not [one of] coherence but [that of] discontinuity. And in a world of discontinuities, contradiction is useless as a test of truth or merit, because contradiction does not exist.
>
> My point is that we are by now so thoroughly adjusted to the "Now . . . this" world of news—a world of fragments, where events stand alone, stripped of any connection to the past, or to the future, or to other events—that all assumptions of coherence have vanished. And so, perforce, has contradiction. In the context of *no context,* so to speak, it simply disappears. And in its absence, what possible interest could there be in a list of what the President says *now* and what he said

then? It is merely a rehash of old news, and there is
nothing interesting or entertaining in that. The
only thing to be amused about is the bafflement of
reporters at the public's indifference. There is an
irony in the fact that the very group that has taken
the world apart should, on trying to piece it together again, be surprised that no one notices
much, or cares.

    For all his perspicacity, George Orwell would
have been stymied by this situation; there is nothing "Orwellian" about it. The President does not
have the press under his thumb. *The New York
Times* and *The Washington Post* are not *Pravda;* the
Associated Press is not Tass. And there is no New-
speak here. Lies have not been defined as truth
nor truth as lies. All that has happened is that the
public has adjusted to incoherence and been
amused into indifference. Which is why Aldous
Huxley would not in the least be surprised by the
story. Indeed, he prophesied its coming. He believed that it is far more likely that the Western
democracies will dance and dream themselves into
oblivion than march into it, single file and man-
acled. Huxley grasped, as Orwell did not, that it is
not necessary to conceal anything from a public
insensible to contradiction and narcotized by technological diversions. Although Huxley did not
specify that television would be our main line to
the drug, he would have no difficulty accepting
Robert MacNeil's observation that "Television is
the *soma* of Aldous Huxley's *Brave New World."*
Big Brother turns out to be Howdy Doody [Post-
man, 1985, p. 110].

If individualism and TV were the only forces operating
in U.S. society, then the prospects for change and for economic
survival would indeed be bleak. Fortunately, there are other
forces that, although currently not as powerful, are beginning to

grow. One of the most positive examples is the increasing cooperation between business and education.

The University of Alabama, the United Auto Workers (UAW), and the General Motors (GM) Tuscaloosa carburetor assembly plant have joined together in a unique experiment (Risen, 1985; for a more complete treatment of this experiment, see Campbell and others, 1985). In 1982, GM announced that it planned to close its Tuscaloosa facility. At that time, the auto industry was facing its worst slump in 50 years. The Tuscaloosa facility in particular was losing money and the market for carburetors had collapsed. The tragedy was the loss of another 200 jobs in a state that already had an unemployment rate of 14.4 percent.

GM reluctantly made the decision to close the plant, but only after the plant had been given every opportunity to cut costs. Even though workers and management were able to save an additional 1.5 million dollars, GM's top management decided that they were still $470,000 short of what was required to make the plant profitable and hence sustainable on its own. At the last minute the university, GM, and UAW, persuaded by local business leaders, decided to see if together they could achieve the additional savings required. The plant was designated as an "applied research facility." It was to be open to the university for three years, during which time the university would attempt to find the $470,000. In return for the university's help, GM agreed to give the university $250,000 a year in the form of scholarships, grants, and fellowships. To pay for all of this, the workers agreed to take an approximately 10 percent pay cut. This translated to roughly $55.20 per week per worker, a not insignificant amount for workers by any means.

The project was so successful that it produced the necessary savings in one year, not three. In fact, potential savings of $1.2 million were identified. The workers have been reimbursed for their lost wages, and the total employment at the plant has actually risen from 200, when the project started, to 240 today. Risen (1985) summarizes the means used to achieve the savings: "[University] engineers . . . suggested energy savings, less expensive package designs, and did research on how to use more

computer-aided technology in designing the plant's newest operations. Business professors . . . thought up ways to cut inventory and freight costs, while legal experts from the law school
. . . found less costly ways for [GM's plant] to meet federal
emissions standards on its carburetors. Criminal justice faculty
members . . . advised on improving the cost-efficiency of plant
security, and the medical school has been offering help to set up
a new group health program" [p. 5].

In addition to financial support for research, the university received something even more valuable. It was provided with
a real-world site in which to test academic theories. Although all
parties have suffered considerable strain and conflict, they have
nonetheless benefited from the project. For GM, a valuable
plant has proved even more valuable. The plant not only increased its profits on its traditional product (carburetors), but,
far more important, it learned to manufacture new products
when the carburetors were phased out. The workers not only
saved their jobs but began to learn new jobs. And finally, the
university discovered how to learn in a new type of research
setting.

Although the GM/UAW/University of Alabama joint project may not be an experiment of the magnitude of the Saturn
project, it is an important example of cooperation among diverse institutions. It demonstrates that groups that traditionally
have been at extreme odds with one another can learn to bridge
their differences. It is hard to imagine three groups that have
been more suspicious of, and hence hostile to, one another than
education, labor, and management. Any project that shows the
promise of healing such deep-seated divisions is worth reporting.
The project also illustrates the kind of cooperation that will
have to multiply a thousandfold if this country is to regain its
competitive edge.

And yet because they are so important, it is imperative
that the lessons of the Tuscaloosa experiment be made absolutely clear. Cooperation on economic matters *is possible* in American society but, apparently, *only after* things have reached a
crisis. Thus, we predict that conditions will worsen substantially
before the United States considers such "radical" proposals as

industrial policy. (On the positive side, such venerable publications as *Business Week* seem to have recognized our present condition and have given prominent editorial space to those espousing an industrial policy [Jonas, 1986, pp. 84-85].)

As we have stressed repeatedly, the United States is a victim of its own enormous successes, not failures. It is extremely difficult to realize that what made for success in the past is largely responsible for our current troubles. The pain level will have to rise substantially before we learn that we cannot solve today's problems with the solutions of the past.

Given that human beings are fundamentally not rational creatures, there may be no other way to induce fundamental social change than by pain and suffering. As we look at the great societies of the world, we see no other model of change that has really proved effective (Tuchman, 1984). We wish we were wrong.

8

The New Logic
of the Global Economy:
When Less Can Be More
and More Can Be Less

"A radical back-to-basics movement in computer design has touched off a race to build a new generation of high-performance computers. Instead of championing ever more complex machines, advocates of Risc, for reduced instruction set computing, argue the virtues of computers with simpler circuitry. Risc supporters . . . claim that computers with stripped-down instruction sets zip through programs like racing cars, two or three times faster than ordinary models.

"The proposition that *less might yield much more* [emphasis ours] is so compelling that nearly a dozen companies are pressing ahead with Risc technology, which involves both the design of a chip and the way chips are linked.

"But Risc is mainly controversial because it flies in the face of a longstanding trend toward building more and more operating instructions into computers" (Gannes, 1985, p. 98).

Executive Summary

Old Organizing Assumptions	*New Organizing Assumptions*
1. Growth and the benefits it brings are limitless.	1. Growth and the benefits it brings are limited; at

Old Organizing Assumptions	*New Organizing Assumptions*
	some point, the benefits turn back on themselves and lead to their opposite.
2. "Bigger or more is better" is the fundamental principle governing progress.	2. "Less can be more" is the newly emerging principle of progress.
3. Phenomena obey either the principle "more leads to more" or the principle "less leads to less."	3. Global phenomena are so complex that they fall *simultaneously* into four categories: "more can lead to more," "more can lead to less," "less can lead to less," and "less can lead to more."
4. The ability to manage is equivalent to the ability to eliminate or reduce paradox.	4. The ability to manage all global phenomena is equivalent to the ability to manage paradox; to eliminate or reduce paradox is to fundamentally distort the basic phenomena with which one must deal.

In 1946, Albert Einstein saw clearly that the invention of nuclear weapons had ushered in the most profound change in perhaps all of human history. At the heart of his concern was the deep fear that our basic ways of thinking had failed to keep pace with the revolution in human affairs that nuclear weapons had effected. In the following famous and often quoted statement, Einstein expressed his concern: "The unleashed power of the atom has changed everything save our modes of thinking and we thus drift toward unparalleled catastrophe."

What Einstein could not have anticipated, but, we suspect, would not be surprised to learn were he alive today, is that the changes in thinking that he saw as necessary to deal with the question of nuclear war are the very same changes in thinking necessary to deal with all of the problems discussed in this book. That is, the "patterns of thinking" that are needed to

make sense of nuclear weapons are the same patterns that are
needed to comprehend the global economy (Mitroff, 1986).
The reason, as Reich (1985) has noted in a recent article in *The
Atlantic Monthly,* is that the whole planet is now so interconnected that it has become virtually impossible to say where
"public" issues, such as national security, leave off and "private" issues, such as managing a corporation, take over. Increasingly, we are beginning to understand that there is an intimate
connection between defense and fiscal policies, between strategies for nuclear defense and strategies for industrial development. In this chapter our purpose is to reinforce one last time
the difference in thinking that is required. To do this we extend
the methods discussed in Chapter Three by building on the previous chapters.

More Is Not Always Better

According to ordinary thinking, or, better yet, the reasoning that was appropriate for the world in simpler times,
more or bigger of anything desirable was always better. Thus, if
an organization produced a 15 percent return on initial investment (ROI) in one year or quarter, then it would be better off
if it produced an even greater ROI, say 20 percent, in the next
year or quarter. Unrestricted growth, particularly of something
that could be quantified—hence, the bottom line—was better,
everything else being equal. Thus, growth became an obsession
in itself. The generic expression that best captures the nature of
this relationship is "more of something initially thought to be
desirable leads to something else thought to be just as or even
more desirable." Briefly, "more leads to more."

The simple relationship "more leads to more" has been
the normal order of things, or "business as usual," up to recent
times. In fact, the complementary patterns of reasoning, "more
is more" and "less is less," have governed thinking about war
and other phenomena in our civilization for so long. The first is
the familiar "bigger is better." The second is the just as familiar
"weakness leads to weakness." One can surely appreciate how
applicable these patterns were in simpler times. If you had ten

archers and I had only five, then, all other things being equal, your ten would be superior to my five because if five archers from each side annihilated each other, you would still have five archers to threaten me with. Just as critical, the arrows from your archers' bows would not reverse in flight to impale those who shot them.

Global phenomena, which nuclear weapons represent, have changed all of this drastically. It is not clear that the side with "greater" weapons is "ahead" if both sides possess weapons that are lethal, that is, globally destructive (Mitroff, 1986). In effect, a boomerang point is reached. At a certain point, "more" weapons lead not to "more" but to "less" felt security (Mitroff, 1986). The pattern "more leads to less" thus represents the breakdown of the pattern "bigger is better," which has governed our civilization for so long. It represents nothing less than the shift from a pattern of thinking appropriate for a world conceived in the image of a machine, that is, the world of the Industrial Revolution, to a pattern of thinking appropriate for a complex, interconnected world. For the former world, "bigger is better" was appropriate. Bigger input into the machine (more resources, money, and so on) did lead to bigger output (more products, greater productivity, higher quality of life, and so on). Today, we increasingly find the reverse on every level of our society.

One of the most interesting examples of the breakdown of old patterns of reasoning is found in the world of business. This example, which consists of two different but related features of the banking system, illustrates as well as any example we know the new global dimensions of business. Both features powerfully illustrate that "more of something initially thought to be good in and of itself can actually lead to something undesirable." The first is the Federal Deposit Insurance Corporation, or FDIC; the second is the acceptable ratio of capital to assets that banks are required to keep on hand to cover bad loans. Originally established to stabilize the banking system, these features can actually do just the opposite in today's environment (Hiltzik, 1985; Jones and others, 1985; Kramer, 1984; McComas, 1985). FDIC, which no one denies is a good thing for small depositors because it insures their bank accounts up to $100,000, can actually have the unintended and undesirable side effect of turning what would have been small bank failures into large ones: "With today's de facto unlimited coverage, the rational large depositor has little reason to care how risky his bank is. Indeed, he is rewarded for supporting the highest-risk banks, since he reaps the benefits in the form of the higher-yields such banks have to pay to attract deposits. Meanwhile, the cost—the great probability of failure—is borne by [FDIC]. . . . Deposit insurance largely negates the market's normal safety mechanism—the reduction in credit availability for companies perceived as exceptionally risky—until a bank reaches the edge of the precipice. The effect is to transform what would have been small bank failures into big ones" (Kramer, 1984, p. 136).

The problem is anything but trivial. The risk of bank failure is at its highest level since the Great Depression. Thirty-four commercial banks failed in 1982, 45 in 1983. This compares with averages of 10 a year in the period 1975–1981 and 4.2 a year in the preceding two decades.

Modern technology ("more" of a supposed good thing), which is helping the banking industry manage better in a complex world, is also working against it to produce "less": "The real menace is not the old-line money broker but a new breed . . . called 'deposit spreaders.' These are firms with *computer software* [italics ours] enabling them to parcel multimillion-dollar sums into $100,000 segments—small enough to qualify for full [FDIC] insurance—and spread them across the country to banks offering the highest yields. Not surprisingly, many of those banks rank high on the FDIC's problem bank list" (Kramer, 1984, p. 139).

Although the resolution of this problem is not yet known, one thing is clear. The problem of the banking industry is *systemic*, that is, it involves the *whole system* of banking. Hence, the resolution, if one is to be found, must be systemic as well.

In the world conceived of as a machine, and a simple one at that, it was appropriate to use single numbers to measure, presumably accurately, the performance of separate parts of the system. In the complex world in which we now live, this is no longer possible. In a complex system such as computerized banking, wherein one can scour the country to choose the most advantageous *coordinated package* of deals, one can manipulate single measures of performance. Thus, no matter how desirable they are on the surface, single measures will not benefit the system as a whole.

The second feature, requiring banks to keep more capital in reserve to cover potentially bad loans, also can produce unintended, negative side effects, that is, more and riskier bad loans. Raising the capital-to-asset ratio from 5.5 to 6.0 percent as proposed could actually encourage banks to make risky investments to generate the profits that would be required to compensate for the tied-up capital. Again, the problem is nothing less than global, as illustrated in a recent article in *Fortune:* "Any increase in the ratio . . . puts banks at a further competitive disadvantage. Currently, thrift institutions are required to have a capital-asset ratio of only 3%. Though they are in a weaker position than the banks—so weak that the regulators are loath to demand more capital at present—the fact is that they compete with banks for a growing proportion of the lending business. The handicap U.S. banks carry in the international arena is even more pronounced. Their counterparts in Japan and France have capital assets of 1% to 3%" (McComas, 1985, p. 82). How many more banks will fail before we realize that all problems are truly systemic or global and, as such, will be resolved only by systemic or global solutions?

If old patterns of thinking are breaking down because they are no longer effective in managing today's problems, then a new pattern is emerging that does appear to be effective: "less can lead to more." That is, "small can be beautiful." It is a standard that is based in part on the ideas of the late economist E. F. Schumacher, author of the best-selling book *Small Is Beautiful: Economics as if People Mattered* (1973). Instead of an uncritical acceptance of sheer growth or of "bigger is better," advocates of this position claim that what matters most in any relationship is quality. Quality, in business as in anything, is the continual development of the capability to improve one's quality of life. Many businesses have realized this and have thus deliberately refused to grow for the sake of growth alone. Thus, for instance, WQED public television, producer of the award-winning National Geographic Specials, has steadfastly refused to increase the number of shows (four) it makes each season, despite considerable and continual pressures to do so. WQED instinctively knows that it is better to keep the audience wanting more than to saturate its appetite. They know that in quality television programming "less is definitively more."

The same lesson is beginning to dawn on manufacturers. For instance, U.S. auto manufacturers have had to learn, painfully, it might be noted, what their European and Japanese counterparts have known for years: in building cars "less or smaller cars can certainly be more" with regard to the changing life-styles of consumers.

Russell Ackoff, one of the most perceptive business analysts around today, has succinctly contrasted growth and development or quality: "cemeteries grow each year but they don't develop." To which we might add, so do trash heaps, toxic waste dumps, and nuclear arsenals.

The two contrasting patterns, "more leads to more" and "more leads to less," may sound theoretical or academic but the phenomena they represent are anything but that. As stated in a front-page feature article of the *Los Angeles Times,*

> If [the] Campbell [Soup Co.] was to survive in the increasingly aggressive food industry and beat back competition from a new entrant, the Japanese, [then Campbell's CEO] McGovern knew he had to untangle the red tape that was slowing decision making to a crawl and get the nation's biggest soup company quickly back in shape.
>
> "There was only one way to respond, in an entrepreneurial way," McGovern says. "We had to get the company fractured up into small businesses, put people in charge and tell them to get busy."
>
> Like Campbell, hundreds of America's large corporations have been forced by external pressures into an urgent reassessment of how they do

> business. And in large numbers they are concluding
> . . . that this very organizational structure that
> served them so well in mature, stable markets was
> inhibiting their ability to adapt and compete in to-
> day's environment of fast changing technology, in-
> tense foreign competition and slow growth.
>   . . . The anatomy of the big American corpo-
> ration is being redesigned [Whitefield, 1985, p. 1].

The preceding thus demonstrates that some of the best firms are learning some critical lessons. They are learning not only that often "more leads to less" but also that in many circumstances, "less or smaller can lead to more." But lest we be misled, we must be very careful to interpret the pattern "less can be more" in its proper sense. "Less can be more" is not a license for organizations to fragment themselves into small, isolated segments as they did in the past (see Chapter Four). Division of large organizations into smaller parts to facilitate management and competition does not mean that the parts can exist or proceed independent of the central organization. If anything, it means that each part has to function with a greater understanding of the entire corporation and global economy. In short, "less is more" does *not* mean that "less does not require a broader, global vision and a greater sense of how the whole functions." Nothing could be further from the truth or more dangerous to believe in today's global business climate.

Although we earlier hinted at the reason for the breakdown of the "more leads to more" pattern, it bears repeating. In a huge, complex world, there are unpredictable forces that interfere with the actions on a system (input) and the resultant effects (output). Too many complicating factors exist in the environment for a simple pattern like "more leads to more" to operate without exception. This should not paralyze the decision maker; however, it does mean that he or she must learn to think broadly to ascertain all the forces of potential impact on the modern corporation. Otherwise, the corporation will be the blind victim of those forces. It is true that one can never know the environment with certainty. It does *not* thereby follow that one should know nothing or not take as broad a view as is humanly possible. Again, we are the prisoners of the machine-age view of knowledge: without complete knowledge of the workings of the machine, one has no knowledge.

The systems age has changed all of this. Uncertainty and imperfection are *inherent* features of a complex system and, hence, of knowledge about the system itself. Knowledge and uncertainty do not exist independently and do not even inhibit one another. Rather, new methods and concepts are required that build on imperfection and uncertainty, strange as this may sound. Uncertainty is an opportunity to widen our thinking. (For sources on how to do this, see Linstone, 1984; Mason and Mitroff, 1981; Mitroff, 1983; Mitroff and Kilmann, 1984; Mitroff, Mason, and Barabba, 1983.) We have no alternative but to learn to think—to reason—differently if we are to fashion the creative solutions we need to survive and prosper as a world economic power today.

The Management of Paradox

Extensive study of the paradoxes connected with nuclear strategy reveals that they fall into four principal categories: (1) more is or leads to more; (2) less is or leads to less; (3) more is or leads to less; and (4) less is or leads to more (Mitroff, 1986). Our purpose in this section is to clarify the nature of these categories and to illustrate further why they now apply to all global phenomena such as the world economy.

From their invention, nuclear weapons have presented paradoxes. For instance, it was quickly realized that given the vast destructive power, the only valid reason for possessing nuclear weapons is to prevent their use by the other side. That is, nuclear weapons exist in the physical sense to serve the abstract purpose of nonuse, for actual use would mean the end of humanity. Or, to put it another way, if both sides feel "equally insecure" because of their ability to deliver a lethal blow, then, presumably, both would feel "secure." Thus, "mutual *in*security" guarantees "mutual security."

The extent to which nuclear strategy is affected by paradox is, however, much greater than realized previously: there is *not a single aspect* of nuclear strategy that does not have a significant paradox associated with it (Mitroff, 1986). As a result, *the management of nuclear strategy is equivalent to the management of paradox.* And, by implication, *the management of paradox is critical to the management of the global economy and, indeed, of all global phenomena.* This is why it is so important to understand the patterns of reasoning appropriate for today's environment.

Consider, for example, the paradox that arises through the Strategic Defense Initiative (SDI), better known as Star Wars, the intent of which is security through defensive rather than offensive capability. Innumerable calculations are needed to decide which, and at what point, enemy missiles should be shot down. Thus, it is estimated that SDI will require a computer program ten to one hundred times larger than any that has been written thus far, or approximately *ten to one hundred million* lines of computer instructions. Now, anyone who has ever done so knows that it is virtually impossible to write a computer program, no matter how short, that will work perfectly the first time. Imagine then the "bugs" in a program as huge as ten to one hundred million lines! Here's precisely where the paradox begins to arise.

One way to test the effectiveness of such a computer program is to send up a wave of our own missiles, the trajectories of which are known, and use the program to "shoot" down these missiles. However, to simulate reality (what the Russians would do), the wave would have to be "sizable." Query: How do we assure the Russians that this "simulation" is not a first strike? For "them" (the Russians) to go along with "us" (the United States), "they" would have to trust "us." If trust had existed at the beginning, there would have been no need for Star Wars. Hence, the paradox: The *less* trust there is between us and our adversaries, the *more* we build weapons of *bigger* scope; the resulting complex weapons require *more* extensive tests but such tests necessitate *greater* trust and cooperation between us and our adversaries for their implementation. But why should "they" cooperate with "us" to further a weapon that is to their disadvantage? The attempt to secure a decisive advantage or security through technology alone is self-defeating *because the testing of the resultant technology depends upon trust and cooperation on the part of the adversary, the very thing that was missing in the first place and hence prompted the technology.* If trust and cooperation are absent at the beginning, how do they magically appear subsequently? *No one* has been able to answer this key question satisfactorily.

Star Wars is a prime example of "more leads to less." More of something initially thought to be desirable (a greater defensive shield which precludes presumably having to trust the adversary) leads to secondary effects counter to the proposed benefits (the resultant computer program needed to run a Star Wars is so complex that it requires greater trust, but greater trust is precluded by the whole process itself). That is, whether or not it works, a "greater" defensive shield may leave us in "worse" condition, because it may lessen the initial trust.

Star Wars actually illustrates a deeper, and hence far more significant point. Star Wars, like all global phenomena, falls into all four categories of reasoning simultaneously. Thus, the following four propositions are all plausible, to varying degrees, at the same time:

1. "More leads to more": A larger defensive shield promises the end benefit of more security; it also promises to force the Soviet Union to the bargaining table. (Proposition 1 may backfire and thus lead to less. Also, although proposition 1 may restrain the Soviet Union and force it to the bargaining table, there is a greater chance of error due to breakdown of a complex system; the result would be less for all parties.)

2. "Less leads to less": Less trust breeds larger weapons, which in turn breed less trust.

3. "More leads to less": Larger weapons breed even less trust and/or less felt security.

4. "Less leads to more": Fewer weapons promise more felt security because they do not threaten the other side as much. The opposite side of the argument is that fewer

weapons may encourage the other side to be more aggressive, thus returning to proposition 1 and completing the cycle.

Complex global phenomena do not obey conventional logic or reasoning. They do not fall neatly into simple, mutually exclusive categories. Therefore they cannot be managed by conventional means. Constant scrutiny of those aspects that fall into all four categories simultaneously is required. That is, one cannot manage complex phenomena by looking at only one category. This is precisely what makes today's world so different.

Another feature makes this whole matter considerably more complex. Because global phenomena are complex mixtures of positive *and* negative features, the definitions of "more" and "less" are not constant across all issues. They vary not only from situation to situation but within a particular situation as well. Thus, what is "more" to one stakeholder may be "less" to another. What is desirable to one party may be undesirable to another. Where one party sees only good, another may see only evil. Thus, the semantics are not incidental. That the basic terms are so slippery does not invalidate the categories, but rather further illustrates the complexity of the basic phenomena with which we are dealing. In specific situations, the applicable meanings of "more" and "less" can generally be easily decided.

Consider the following example, which reveals not only the general industrial strategy pursued by the Japanese but also the specific senses of "more leads to more" and "less leads to less" that they have adopted:

> The kaisha [Japanese companies] are often criticized by their Western counterparts for their obsession with market share. But in a growing market, competitive position and the rate at which that position is changing are the most important indices of performance. Increased market share and increased competitive advantage is obtained by preempting market growth with aggressive pricing and

investment policies [this is the specific sense in
which the Japanese have defined "more leads to
more," or "aggressiveness leads to greater market
share"]. A noncompetitive pricing policy and/or
the failure to add sufficient plant and equipment
capacity and human resources will result in a loss
of competitive position ["less leads to less"]. If a
competitive position is allowed to deteriorate substantially the viability of the business will ultimately be threatened ["less will lead to less"] [Abegglen
and Stalk, 1985, p. 45].

The Japanese have also combined two forms of "more leads to
more" and "less leads to less" with a "less is more" principle by
"focusing" their energies in niche markets, thus showing that
total combination of principles is important for an *integrated*
strategy.

Figure 4 is a simple visualization of the phenomena. Look
at the inverted U-shaped curve *ABCD*. The part from *A* to *B*
represents the principle "more leads to more"; that is, greater
input leads to greater output, although at a diminishing rate.
From *B* to *D,* greater input leads to lesser output. And if at
point *C* the output decreases catastrophically, then *CE* would
represent the principle "less input leads to less output." If the
catastrophe is such that recovery is made, then *EF* would represent "less leads to more." Ideally, if point *C* is sensed before
point *B* is reached, a switch to *BG,* or "less leads to more,"
could be made, thereby avoiding the catastrophe.

Note that whatever course is followed, the entire process
repeats endlessly, because the phenomena with which we are
dealing are dynamic. They never remain the same; they are always developing.

The real world is vastly more complex. Curve *ABCD* is
never fully known. It may have severe ups and downs or breaks.
In such circumstances, the best one can do is to apply the methods discussed in Chapter Three: Continually challenge constraints and assumptions. Eternal vigilance must be the key,
flexible thinking its servant. However much one would like per-

Figure 4. Relationships Among Contrasting Patterns of Reasoning.

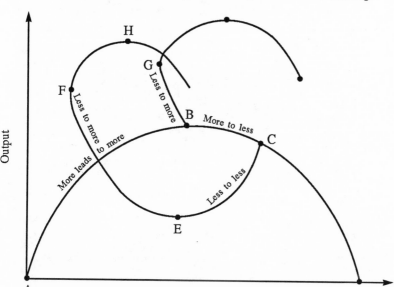

fect solutions, the best one can do is continually cope, but never solve. Although this is frustrating, it provides a great challenge to those who can stand the uncertainty. That is, less certainty can lead to great opportunity for those who are mentally prepared to take advantage of it.

9

The Global Challenge: Designing and Implementing a New Public Philosophy

"[A] new public philosophy would lead to policies that would embrace the new reality of interdependence in all three realms—economics, foreign affairs, and social policy. . . .

". . . Domestic social policy in education, child nutrition and care, job training, and so on would come to be seen as an extension of our policies for global adjustment.

"But none of these piecemeal responses to global interdependence, nor any others, will come about unless they are framed by a new public philosophy. *The relationships are too complex, and the changes they signify too painful, to be accepted without a fundamental shift in how we perceive reality* [italics ours]. What stories will we tell each other to justify and explain this altered world? What parables will help us recognize and accept the new patterns? How can we impart new meanings to the ideas of prosperity and security, on a planet where clear lines can no longer be drawn between *us* and *them?*" (Reich, 1985, p. 79).

Executive Summary

Old Organizing Assumptions	*New Organizing Assumptions*
1. Left alone, we will grow out of the problems we	1. The pain we have already experienced in the decline

Old Organizing Assumptions	*New Organizing Assumptions*
face through the continued application of traditional solutions. In essence, we do not have to change our fundamental social organization to compete internationally.	of our international competitiveness is small compared with the pain we will experience in undertaking the changes necessary to maintain our position.
2. We will not go the way of Great Britain.	2. There is a real possibility that unless we make the necessary changes in time we not only may go the way of Great Britain but may enter a catastrophic decline.
3. We do not need to change substantially.	3. We ultimately will make the changes required and, thereby, avoid a world economic catastrophe.

Throughout this book, we have attempted to document the profound changes taking place all over the world. As the quotation that opens this chapter illustrates, these changes will never be fully accepted unless the reasons for their occurrence are first comprehended. As Reich so rightly argues, this comprehension must be grounded in a new perception of reality. It must be understood that the structure of the world has changed drastically. The world can no longer be envisioned as a simple machine. It must be understood as nothing less than a complex, highly interconnected, global system.

This new comprehension must occur at more than the intellectual level. It must also involve a readjustment of our ethics and aesthetics to the new unfolding pattern of reality. This helps to explain why we are experiencing so much difficulty in adjusting to the new order. We are required to adjust, simultaneously, to profound changes occurring at three different but related aspects of social reality: intellectual, ethical, and aesthetic. In this chapter, we attempt to tie together these three strands of social reality: a new intellectual perception of the emerging world, an ethic that makes sense of it, and an aesthetic appreciation of it. Because this design is constantly evolving, we can illustrate it only in broad strokes.

Four Scenarios

Figure 4 (Chapter Eight) is reproduced here as Figure 5 to illustrate four very different scenarios for the future development of the United States:

I.   Continually increasing prosperity without substantial change or dislocation (curve AB).
II. Continued prosperity with substantial early adjustment (curve $A\ B^1\ C^1$).
III. Late and slow recovery only after substantial pain (curve $A\ B^2\ C^2\ D^2$).
IV. Catastrophic decline after severe pain (curve $A\ B^3\ C^3$).

Figure 5. Four Future Scenarios for the United States.

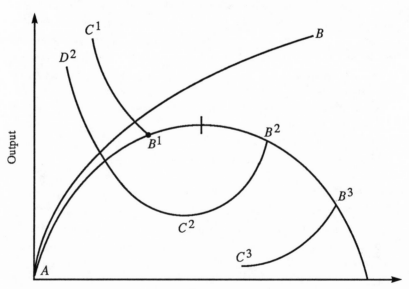

Input

Scenario I is obviously the most optimistic scenario that could be formulated. Basically it assumes that past methods of operation are sound and will lead to increasing prosperity in the foreseeable future. Thus, under scenario I we don't need to change our basic thinking about complex problems, we don't need to restructure our organizations and industries, and, above all, we don't need an integrated industrial policy (IP) to compete in the world economy. Scenario I thus reflects a variation of the "bigger is better" principle: "more of what was successful in the past will produce more success in the future." Hence, scenario I is based on the following assumptions: A free market is the best way to regulate a complex economy. If the economy isn't working the way it should then the government must be at fault; therefore, government must reduce its role. There must be a substantial shift of programs from the public to the private sector. Trade imbalances are primarily the result of the unfair trade practices of other nations. And the huge national debt is the result of excessive spending for welfare and other social programs. For the reasons we have given throughout this book, we believe that scenario I and its underlying assumptions are, at best, wishful thinking. At worst, and the worst occurs daily, it delays the necessary changes and, thus, could propel us unwitting into scenario IV, the most pessimistic scenario.

Scenario II is also optimistic but in a very different way. Its basic premise is a *highly adaptive America*. Scenario II assumes that the United States has seen enough clear signals of the decline of its industries to begin to make the shift to new patterns (for example, less bureaucratic, smaller, more autonomous companies that can compete more effectively in world markets). There are parts of American industry for which this scenario holds, for example, the new, mini steel mills; however, as we noted in Chapter Six, even these are in trouble, for no industry can fully compete without overall policies at the national level. In our view, the spell of scenario I is still too strong to be broken.

Scenario III is optimistic in yet a different way. It predicts that *substantial pain* will occur before the United States finally makes the changes necessary to compete in a world economy.

That is, many more industries will reach "near death" before
the wall of resistance that has been built on past successes is
broken down and they realize that radical restructure is critical
to survival, let alone prosperity.

Scenario IV, the most pessimistic, maintains that by the
time the pain has become so great that change is wanted, it will
be too late. Foreign products and competitors will have made
such a dent in our domestic markets, not to mention world markets, that the chance of disengaging their stronghold will be nil.
Scenario IV is pessimistic in other ways, too. In the early 1970s,
the United States became dependent on cheap foreign oil to
pull the economy out of various recessions. The economy has
also become dependent on the infusion of substantial foreign
capital to recover from the downturns of recent years. In the
same vein, given that the percentage savings of the U.S. population (5 percent in 1983) is low (for example, compared with that
of the Japanese, 21 percent in 1983, our primary competitors),
foreign capital has been used to finance expansion and renova-
tion. Although showing signs of trouble, the U.S. economy is still
one of the strongest in the world. Further, the high interest rates
obtainable in the United States ensure a better return on investment. The great disaster looming on the horizon is that the foreign investors will have to be paid back someday. Foreign debt
is not like internal debt, which can be delayed, or forgiven, if
agreement is reached. The case with foreign debt is entirely different, as Thurow (1985a) has stated:

> International debts are much more serious than na-
> tional debts. With international debts all of the lia-
> bilities are held by Americans and all of the assets
> are held by foreigners. Foreign debts are by defini-
> tion owed to foreigners—not other Americans. As a
> consequence foreign debts represent a direct one-
> for-one future (but no one knows exactly when)
> reduction in American standards of living. By the
> very fact that foreigners have accumulated a net
> creditor position vis-à-vis the United States, they
> have accumulated the right at some future point in

time to come to Americans and demand repay-
ment. At that point the goods and services that are
necessary to make those repayments must be taken
away from Americans and given to foreigners. Foreigners have accumulated that right since they are
today giving Americans goods and services that
Americans have not paid for. There are relatively
few ways that today's Americans can place burdens
on tomorrow's Americans, but the accumulation of
international debt is one of them.

Today's solution to the deficit in the balance
of payments—debt accumulation—is not a long-run
answer to America's competitive problems. If
Americans cannot build products foreigners want
to buy, Americans will ultimately be forced to accept a lower standard of living. In this case "forced"
means that the value of the dollar will fall and that
foreign goods and services will become more and
more expensive as far as Americans are concerned
[p. 92].

And as Fallows (1985b) adds,

Because of the deficits, the government needs to
borrow more money; because it has borrowed
more, real interest rates have gone up; because U.S.
interest rates are higher, foreigners are depositing
more money in American banks; and because so
much foreign money has been coming into the
country, the exchange rate for the dollar became
and has stayed unreasonably high. By most estimates, the dollar is worth about 40 percent more
than its "natural" value against European and Japanese currencies. This is the equivalent of a 40 percent export tax on U.S. products, and it has had
predictable results.

. . . For a variety of reasons—lack of investment opportunities in their own countries, persis-

tently high interest rates in the United States, other factors whose influence economists are now debating—[the Japanese] have deposited their dollars in U.S. banks and bought U.S. bonds, rather than trading the dollars for yen. Several consequences have followed. Japanese VCRs and Italian shoes seem artificially cheap in the United States, since the value of the dollar has been held artificially high. Credit is artificially easy for Americans to obtain, since the Bank of America can use the deposits it has received from Japanese investors to make loans to families that want to buy Japanese cars. When all the complications are boiled away, what's left is a cycle in which the United States started borrowing money from foreigners to buy cut-rate foreign goods—and has kept borrowing and buying at faster and faster rates.

By the end of last year the international debts of the United States had grown so quickly that they had come to equal its investments. And they kept on growing; indeed, because of the workings of compound interest they gathered speed as the United States moved deeper into the debtor category. By the end of this year the United States will stand roughly $100 billion in debt to the rest of the world, which will make it the largest debtor nation, eclipsing the Mexicos and Argentinas—and this less than three years after being the largest creditor. By the end of next year it will owe at least $100 billion more [pp. 19-20].

It would be nice indeed if we could predict which scenario will be enacted. But, as we have explained in previous chapters, there is only one kind of world in which such a prediction could be made. The world would have to be a simple machine, the metaphor we no longer see as appropriate. Hence, we think that each scenario captures to different extents the events of a more complex world. If we had to pick one, it would be scenario III. We do believe that the United States will eventually make the changes it needs to compete. That is the "good news." The "bad news" is that given the quick-fix mentality characteristic of our society, the United States will suffer considerable pain before it breaks out of the old patterns.

Finally, lest we be lulled into believing that the preceding scenarios apply only to the United States. or are purely a figment of our imagination, we found, to our pleasant surprise, that the same scenarios have been seen as applicable, in principle, to other societies:

> Recent discussions of the prospects for the Japanese economy fall into two main categories, or scenarios, as outlined in [the table below]. The two possible scenarios outlined have equal credibility. One has the Japanese economy experiencing industrial decline: the country succumbs to affluence with deteriorating work habits and increased government programs to expand welfare and reduce savings and investment. It invests in an expanding and substantial military capability; it fails to make significant progress in industrial research and development; and it fails to deal with the political and fiscal issues that are already serious problems. This is an affluent, mature society and economy that has lost its dynamism but is comfortable with its level of achievement [the "more leads to less" scenario].

Two Scenarios For Japan's Future

Maturity and Industrial Decline [more leads to less]	*Renewed Growth After a Readjustment Period [more leads to less, less leads to less, less or different leads to more]*
Aging population	Moderating welfare increases
Rising welfare costs	Reorganization of tax structure

Maturity and Industrial Decline *[more leads to less]*	*Renewed Growth After a Readjustment Period* *[more leads to less, less leads to less, less or different leads to more]*
Larger government budgets and tax levels	Political redistricting: lower land and agriculture prices
Slowing savings and private investment	and subsidies
Basic industries losing competitiveness	Reorganization of public corporations (Japan National
Inability to innovate and invest	Railroad; Nippon Telephone and Telegraph)
Closing export markets	Automation of conventional manufacture
Competition from NICs (newly industrialized countries)	Shift to higher technologies Heavy foreign investment
Increased military spending	Stimulus from Asian growth Moderate defense expenditure
Low growth and declining competitiveness	Moderate growth in 1980s;
An affluent but static economy	higher growth in 1990s; world economic leader

In the second scenario, Japan emerges as world leader. It succeeds in restructuring its industry; it solves its fiscal crisis by revising tax policies, reorganizing government agencies, and capping its welfare programs; it establishes an independent and substantial R&D capability; and it emerges by the end of the 1980s into another period of high growth driven by major positions in the cutting-edge industries of the world's economy [Abegglen and Stalk, 1985, pp. 39-40].

Note: For an excellent in-depth examination of these scenarios and additional ones, see Hawken, Ogilvy, and Schwartz (1982).

A Parable for Our Times?

In the same sense that a different pattern of reasoning is required for the systems age, different sets of ethics and aesthetics are also required. These different ethics and aesthetics are best illustrated in a parable, the very thing that Reich so rightly contends is needed today. A parable is a medium that directly touches our deepest feelings. The difficulty is that the parable that we think is appropriate is one that many Americans will have trouble in accepting. It goes against the grain of current thinking and contemporary values. And yet, this makes its impact all the greater. Most of all, the parable shows that no society that pretends to greatness can achieve it by stressing economic or survival values alone. Survival, economic utilitarianism, and individualism are not strong enough by themselves to motivate a society to greatness, let alone sustain it. Greatness comes out of deeper stirrings.

The parable is taken from the writings of C. West Churchman, one of the few distinguished philosophers of science who have actually studied and practiced management (1983). It concerns an imaginary conversation between a nineteenth-century buffalo hunter and a twentieth-century lover of nature, or what some would call an ecologist. The conversation takes place on a bluff high above a plain where the hunter once killed a great number of buffalo. The twentieth-century commentator confronts the hunter (we have paraphrased the conversation as follows):

Twentieth-century commentator: You know, Hunter, I can well understand your love of the kill such that you wanted to hunt down and even kill off the buffalo in great numbers. Anyone who doesn't understand this aspect of people is really naive and thoroughly represses the love of the kill—call it even the lust for blood—that resides in all of us. We're still "primitive," if that's even the right word to call the "hunter" side of our complex psyches.

The thing that really saddens me, however, is not just that you killed off almost all the buffalo, but that

you deprived future generations of their "right" to engage in their "lust for blood" if they so desired to exercise it.

Hunter: I can well understand your disappointment, but who
can really fault us for not having looked far enough ahead
to future generations? Surely your generation is no better
in this respect than ours. Look at all the "wonderful presents" you are bequeathing to your children and, even
worse, to their children: toxic pollution that will last for
thousands of years, buried underground or not; the threat
of global destruction, the end of all life as both of us have
known it. Your generation not only invented genocide, a
wholly new crime against all of humanity, but now
you've invented the means to destroy the entire planet.
You've also managed to pass on an incalculable financial
debt of staggering proportions to your progeny. And *you*
accuse *me* of being irresponsible! *You* pretend to lecture
me! How dare you!

Even so, I have a proposal to make to compensate
you for your loss of not being able to engage in the kill
that I so enjoyed. Suppose that I had set up a trust fund
in the nineteenth century to compensate you financially
for your loss in the twentieth. Suppose further that the
fund grew at today's prevailing market rates so that you
and your generation were compensated very well indeed.
Wouldn't this be enough to dampen your disappoint-
ments? After all, aren't there among you today those that
argue that everything is really a matter of economic "trade-
offs"? What are you willing to trade for the "lost opportunity" of not being able to engage in the hunt? Can't
you weigh the "benefits" I'm willing to pay you versus
the "costs" or "lost opportunities" of your not being able
to kill the buffalo as I did?

Twentieth-century commentator: (barely able to contain his
anger and outrage) Look, you're right that considerable
numbers of my generation are no better than yours. I
wouldn't deny this for one moment. *But,* look at the in-

credible *moral* principle that is embedded in your seemingly innocuous principle of economic reasoning, or cost-benefit, trade-off analysis.

The moral principle is: "whenever a generation has the power, resources, or values—call it what you will—to compensate (bribe?) another generation for the wholesale destruction of a species, it has the license, if not the *moral right,* to do so." This is not only incredible but too horrible beyond words to even respond to rationally.

My generation has had to learn (some still have not learned it and probably never will) that the principle certainly does not apply to people. Surely, the principle you have outlined was the reasoning that guided the Nazis in their wholesale destruction of the Jews, Catholics, and other "undesirables" in World War II. But why then does the principle apply any more to species other than us humans? Do the animals of the earth deserve to be governed by such a moral principle any more than humans? Some of us are not so sure, as perhaps you are, that the buffalo is any lesser or lower a creature and therefore deserving of less consideration.

In this regard, there is one lesson that my century learned that represents a decisive advance over yours. We learned to formulate and to pass new kinds of legislation which protected species from wholesale destruction. They are called Endangered Species Acts. I would argue that such acts are more than legislative. They are primarily religious and moral in spirit even if they act under the cover of legislation. They say in effect that certain things are worth preserving irrespective of all economic considerations. To my way of thinking, to put a price tag of any kind on living things is the height of immorality.

The power of the parable surely lies in the extreme contrast it presents between two moral principles. On the one hand, the principle of the nineteenth-century hunter is that values not only have their dollar value but can also be ranked in the form of priorities. On the other hand, the principle of the twentieth-

century systems thinker is that even the attempt to discuss
morality in terms of price is the height of immorality itself. In
other words, the hunter follows the "growth," or "measure-
ment," model of human affairs discussed in Chapter Eight. For
the hunter, only two conditions exist in the world: "more leads
to more" and "less leads to less." After all, if all things are mea-
surable, and if the world follows a clear-cut pattern, then what
one gets back is determined by what one puts in. The twentieth-
century systems practitioner follows the "quality," or "development," model of human affairs. For this person, "more" of
things of monetary value does not automatically lead to more,
in the sense of a better quality of life; rather, "more" often
leads to a lesser quality of life. In this view, "less can often lead
to more."

From a moral point of view, there is a world of difference between these two principles. It is the difference between
evaluating things in terms of dollar value and appreciating
things for their inherent qualities. It is the difference between
adopting a cost-benefit attitude toward the preservation of living things and adopting an endangered species mentality. Indeed, today human beings are the most endangered of all species and, therefore, most needy of an endangered species mentality.

We believe that today the world is in the process of shifting from (1) ethics and aesthetics that reflect uncritical acceptance of unrestricted growth to (2) ethics and aesthetics that
reflect the dysfunctional consequences of unrestricted growth.
The switch is from an ethics and aesthetics that are primarily
utilitarian in their meaning and application to ones that are primarily Kantian in their outlook (Churchman, 1983). Without
going into all the ramifications, suffice it to say that in the context of the issues with which we are dealing, that is, the global
economy, Kantian ethics and aesthetics entail the moral injunc-
tion to consider one's proposed actions from the vantage points
of as many stakeholders as possible. It means considering such
questions as Can one's actions and plans be universalized to all
stakeholders? Will one's actions primarily benefit the most ad-
vantaged actors in a system? Why ought they not to benefit the

most disadvantaged? And finally, Because societies often have the resources to compel limited, restricted views of the world, does that give them the moral right to impose tunnel vision as our society so often seems to do? The unstated moral principle that underlies current society seems to be Whenever a society has the power and the resources to reinforce a limited view of the world, it ought to do so; worse yet, whenever a society has the consent or the power to saddle future generations with a staggering debt, it ought to do so.

If our investigation has taught us anything, it is that "less is more" *may* be the common vision that unites conservatives and liberals if, and only if, both realize that this principle can operate *only* within a broad view of the world. "More is more" and "less is more" actually operate simultaneously in today's world. "Less is more" operates in the sense that "small *can be* beautiful" but does not guarantee it. "More is more" *can* operate but only if it is clearly understood that the world is now so coupled that its management demands a *bigger* picture of reality. Thus, "more" has a different meaning today than in the machine age. *"More" now entails a broader vision—a global vision.*

Today, any view of reality that does not embody an understanding of how these two potentially competing views complement one another is misleading and dangerous. For this reason, we are highly critical of the recent article by Thurow (1985b), a highly able social thinker with whom we generally agree. Thurow argues that because none of the major governmental players in the world economy have either the vision, political will, or courage to make the hard choices required to forge institutions that can manage the global economy, the nations of the world will have to (ought to?) move to a system wherein their economies are decoupled. Now, we do not doubt for one minute the basis of Thurow's decision, only his conclusion. In our view, he ignores the fact that the world's economies are already so integrated, for example, in the strong interdependence observed in electronic financial networks, that decoupling no longer seems possible.

The nations of the world have decisively entered the systems age, whether or not their institutions have. The task, therefore, is not to lower the capabilities of our institutions but to bring them up to meet the demands of the new world. The challenge is to fashion new ethics and aesthetics that are up to the demands of this new world.

Nations, like individuals, can no longer afford to follow the unstated but still strong moral dictum that whenever a nation has the power and the resources to practice tunnel vision, it ought to do so. Using tunnel vision is not only a poor strategy for survival in a complex world but is an ethic and aesthetic vision that can never lead a nation to greatness.

The prime question remains: Can we construct new social ethics (values) that are embedded within the appropriate aesthetics (parable) such that they can inspire the nation to further greatness? Can we truly embrace complexity at a time when more than ever we seek simplicity? If we are fortunate, this will be the first generation in history to learn that it can cope with its economic and social problems only by widening its vision to include the entire world. If we are not fortunate, we will drift further toward unparalleled catastrophe in every dimension of our existence.

10

Epilogue:
The World as a Garden:
A Global Metaphor

"A garden, be it Western or Japanese, is like speech; it is an expression with intention and design. The gardener selects paintings and ornaments that please him, and he arranges them by whatever criteria he feels are important; he may favor function over shape, or color over texture. He is practical and accumulates information before deciding anything; he checks the pH of his soil. . . . On these counts, Western and Japanese gardeners are much the same. Yet the languages their gardens speak are [very] different . . . the language of the Japanese garden—its words . . . are its stones, streams, and plants, and its grammar . . . is the system of arrangement that carries the message" (Seike, Kudo, and Engel, 1980, p. 37).

"A garden is a living thing, and a good garden can only exist when its owner gives it constant care. A garden, in fact, is a mirror that reflects the owner's heart and his family's way of life" (Itoh, 1985, p. 92).

Executive Summary

Old Organizing Assumptions	*New Organizing Assumptions*
1. The world *is* a simple machine.	1. The world *is* a combination of a complex system and a global garden.

Old Organizing Assumptions	*New Organizing Assumptions*
2. Therefore, specialization of functions, hierarchical control, and unilateral communication constitute the best way to organize industrial societies. Autonomy of the parts must be given paramount consideration in the design of an organization.	2. Therefore, the parts of an organization must be arranged so as to stress their extreme interconnectedness: power must be shared; structures must be flat; communication must be two-way. The whole must be given paramount consideration in the design of an organization.

Human beings live by images, myths, and metaphors. We are natural-born imagemakers, mythmakers, and storytellers. In every known epoch, we have used powerful images and stories to give order and purpose to our existence.

In this final chapter, we examine four basic images of the world. We show how each has dictated our concept of the corporation and its relationship to other organizations and to the environment.

The World as a Simple Machine

The oldest image of the world, that of a simple machine, pervades and still dominates much of economic and managerial science. This viewpoint is classically expressed by economist Milton Friedman, although it is also scattered throughout the literature of the economic and managerial sciences. According to this view, the modern corporation can be partitioned into three primary entities: the corporation itself, its stockholders, and its customers (see Figure 6). The reason most often given is that the primary purpose of management (presumably the upper echelons of the corporation) is to serve the primary actor in their environment, that is, the stockholder. All other interested parties either do not exist or are not recognized as significant. At a minimum, this view assumes that the rest of the environment can be separated from the three stakeholders in Figure 6.

Figure 6. The World as a Simple Machine.

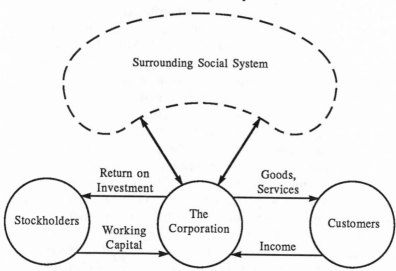

As many have noted, among them most prominently Ackoff (1981) and Toffler (1980), this view of the world is founded on the taken-for-granted metaphor of the world as a simple machine. As such, it derives, as we discussed in Chapter Two, from the Industrial Revolution, where human beings, animals, plants, and the environment were conceived of in mechanical terms.

Because, by definition, a machine can be separated into its components, analysis, or reductionism, was and still is the favored mode of study from this viewpoint. A natural outcome was the partitioning of the universe into distinct causes and effects. From the standpoint of scientific methodology, this philosophy was classically expressed in the work of John Stuart Mill (1872). Today everything that is labeled experimental design is a direct outgrowth of Mill's canons of induction. If the world is not a machine then this restricts the use of experimentation as a method of learning appropriate for the applied social sciences (Mitroff, 1974, 1983; Mitroff and Kilmann, 1978).

Because, also by definition, a machine is an object, that is, it has no emotions, its workings can be described in purely impersonal terms. Hence, economics became and still is the natural language with which to describe (better yet, "represent") the workings of society and organizations. Or, to be more accurate, the *brand* of economics we developed was suited to this representation, that is, a brand that recognizes only the ego component of the human psyche as valid and therefore views people as rational calculating devices, making all their decisions on the strict basis of benefits versus cost calculations alone. If this supposition is true of all people, then the behavior of and between individuals can be described as series of impersonal economic transactions. Furthermore, because egos are supposedly separable from one another, the properties of each individual may in principle also be separable from the rest of the system. To be sure, how individuals behave is a function of the rest of the system, but supposedly their internal constitutional properties are not. Thus, in principle, the individual could be removed from the surrounding system and studied in isolation.

The concept of productivity that this image of the world warrants follows directly from it. Productivity is that which affects the economic welfare of the single actor or ego, the stockholder. Further, as befitting the limited concept of the ego that is inherent in this picture, productivity is measured in the most limited of terms. Productivity is measured in machinelike terms, that is, the *ratio* of the *output* in goods and services *generated* to the *input* in capital, materials, or energy *invested.*

Given the complexity of the environment in which modern corporations now operate, this image of the world and the concept of productivity that follows from it are no longer adequate. Both grossly misrepresent the nature of the forces that drive human beings, both ignore complexity, and both trivialize human behavior. In short, mechanistic conceptions of human nature and organizational performance are two of the principal forces responsible for the current ill health of many of our organizations.

The World as a Complex System

In the 1950s, the image of the world as a simple machine, which as a result of the extreme influence of the Industrial

Revolution had so long dominated our collective imagination, seriously began to crumble (Ackoff, 1981). Cybernetics and other methods of describing complex systems with intricate interdependencies and feedback loops were developed. Along with these developments, which continue to this day, came the recognition that the world was a highly complex system of interconnected elements, not a simple machine of largely independent entities. It was only a matter of time before this recognition spread to organizations (see Figure 7). The modern corporation realized that it was increasingly buffeted by a growing number of constantly shifting players in a complex system. This set of players can be called *stake*holders (Ackoff, 1981; Mason and Mitroff, 1981). In contrast to the single class of

Figure 7. The World as a Complex System.

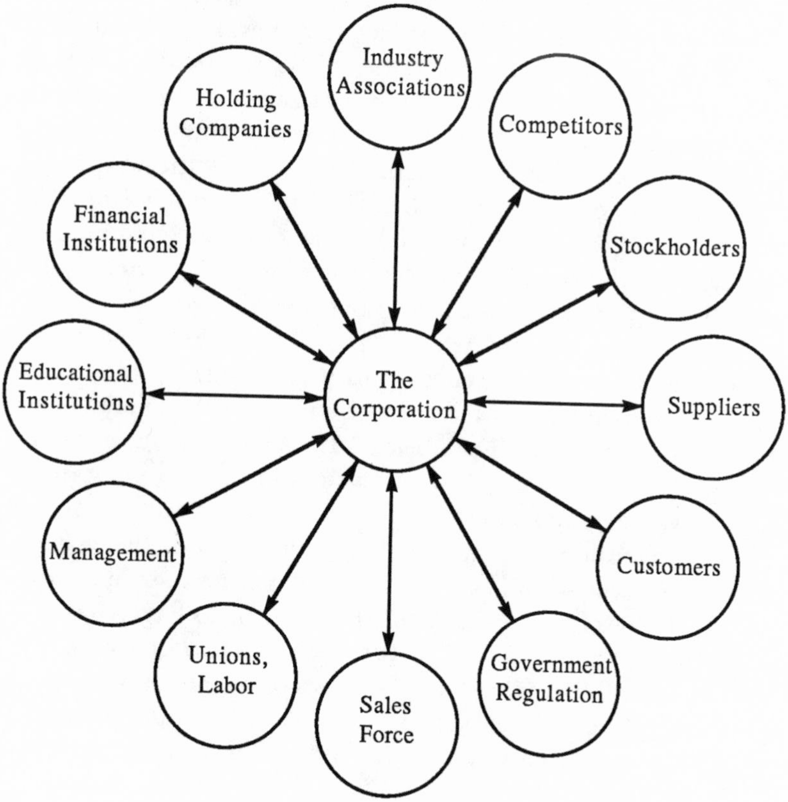

*stock*holders, still vitally important to be sure, *stake*holders are all those vested-interest groups (institutions and individuals) who either affect or are affected by an organization's policies and behavior. It is important to appreciate that this view of the world differs from the preceding one because it contains more parties and because the interrelationships among these parties are very different. As to the first difference, the modern corporation has no choice but to recognize that it must contend with the largest-ever set of external forces whether or not it agrees with these forces. As to the second, in the view of the world as a complex system, in principle none of the stakeholders can be described independently from the entire system of which they are parts (Ackoff, 1981; Mitroff, 1983). The properties of each stakeholder are not self-contained. Different stakeholders not only have more and more impact on the surface behavior of one another but, increasingly, they also intrude more and more deeply into the internal properties (psyches, if you will) of all stakeholders. That is, the properties of all those stakeholders external to the organization affect more and more the properties of those stakeholders internal to the organization.

An even more apt metaphor is that of "the world as an organism" (Ackoff, 1981; Mitroff, 1983). To take a simple example, the heart and the eye neither exist nor function separately from the brain or the rest of the body—the whole system of which they are parts. The human being is not an organization, that is, a system whose "parts" have independent and therefore separate existences and wills. Rather, the human physical constitution is a whole system. So is the human behavioral constitution. A human being is not self-contained but rather is dependent on the larger social system for his or her existence, beliefs, values, and so forth.

It should also be noted that both images of the world, as a complex system and as a simple machine, share some features. Both view interactions between stakeholders as largely rational. In both images we are still at the egoistic or surface level of social analysis (Mitroff, 1983). To be sure, the image of the complex system recognizes the existence, or even more basic, the right to exist, of more parties with a hold on the modern corporation, but it is still limited in the number of parties deep within the psyches of individuals and of institutions that it recognizes. For this reason, the second picture can still be called "the world as a complex but rational (that is, economic) system."

We can only mention in passing the methods of analysis that the complex-system view promotes. Because synthesis of parts into ever-encompassing wholes is the main premise of this view, we should not be surprised to find that methods that are founded on the reduction of the world into smaller and smaller atoms are viewed with extreme suspicion if not disfavor. Instead, methods that attempt to aid the imagination to envision the whole system, of which any component must necessarily be a part, are promoted (Ackoff, 1981; Mason and Mitroff, 1981). That is, as much emphasis is placed on the connections between parts as on the parts themselves.

To summarize, in dealing with complex systems it may be more important to identify as many different potential stakeholders as possible and to outline broadly the nature of the potential interactions (assumptions) than to know the behavior of any particular stakeholder in excruciating detail. Because certainty is not accorded the same exalted status in the complex-system picture as in the simple-machine picture, bringing different views of the social system to the table for explicit debate is regarded as more important than holding with certainty one view of a complex social system. Thus, for greater accuracy Figure 7 should be regarded not as a single picture but as a montage (complex social system) comprising many different pictures (stakeholders). In principle, there are as many different pictures of Figure 7 as there are different stakeholders within any given picture. Little wonder why experimentation *within* any particular picture is *not* given as much weight as examination of the assumptions *between* pictures that warrant belief in any particular picture. Hence, the importance of methods for examining assumptions, as Chapters Three and Five stressed.

The concept of productivity that follows from this picture is systemic. The productivity of an individual or organization is not identified with any single measure of productivity, no matter how intuitively appealing it may be. Further, the productivity of neither an individual nor an organization is identified with one of its parts exclusively. From this standpoint, productivity cannot be measured in economic or technical terms alone. For instance, what profits an organization in the broad sense if it benefits its stockholders maximally but at the expense of the ill-health of disadvantaged stakeholders? The productivity of an organization or of a stakeholder for that matter cannot be discussed apart from the larger system of which it is an integral part. From the perspective of this image, the concept of a "healthy or productive *part*" of something so complex as an organization has virtually no meaning at all. For a vivid example at the national level, see *The 1980 Census: Policy Making amid Turbulence* (Mitroff, Mason, and Barabba, 1983).

This concept does not go far enough. Although it recognizes technical complexity, it does not necessarily recognize deep emotional complexity. As a result, the concept of organizational and human productivity that this image warrants is still limited.

In this image of the world, productivity is first conceptualized, and only then measured, from diverse, and even competing, standpoints. This image then tries to reconcile, if possible, the diverse notions into an overall measure of *systemic* performance. Being productive from this standpoint consists of being aware of diverse measures of performance and of relating the performance of each part to the whole, and vice versa. Thus in this image, productivity is much more of an intellectual feat than it is the production of simple material items. If this is so, we have hit upon the reason it is becoming less and less appropriate to transfer the concepts of productivity appropriate to the machine age to the highly complex, interdependent world of today.

The World as a Complex Hologram

Figure 8 adds a number of things that Figure 7 does not contain. First, it adds a number of stakeholders that Figure 7 ignores. For the most part these additional characters derive

Figure 8. The World as a Complex Hologram.

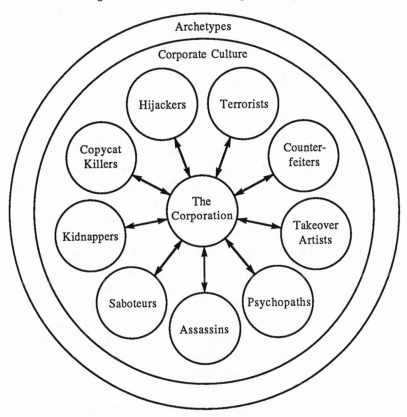

from general psychoanalytic thought (Wilber, 1981) and from the study of psychopathic and sociopathic behavior in particular (Mitroff, 1983; Mitroff and Kilmann, 1984).

Recent acts against corporations, such as the placing of poison in Tylenol, demonstrate that the term "stakeholder," if it is confined to such parties as suppliers, salespeople, customers, and the like, is inadequate (Mitroff and Kilmann, 1984). The traditional concept of stakeholders is far too limited and benign to capture the range of evil and bizarre characters that now affect modern corporations. Thus, the additional characters surrounding the inner circle represent the impact of these other stakeholders on the corporation.

For the most part, the stakeholders indicated in Figure 7 represent the impact of stakeholders, at the sociological or institutional level, on the corporation. This level is not wrong; it is merely incomplete. Figure 8 adds another set of stakeholders which emanates from impulses that are rooted in the human psyche (Wilber, 1981). (See Mitroff [1983] for an analysis of the different social "laws" that "stakeholders" at different levels of social reality obey.)

Figure 8 is meant to indicate that *all* of the stakeholders in Figures 7 and 8 are potentially in contact with one another. When people either individually or in institutions interact with one another, they do more than merely engage in impersonal economic transactions. The human being is more—much, much more—than a mere economic calculating machine. We possess more than an ego. We also possess an id and a superego, Freud would say, and a complex archetypal structure, according to Jung. The point is that whenever two people of two institutions interact with one another they do more than merely exchange goods or services. They exchange something far deeper. They form images of one another. They project their hopes, fears, dreams, wishes, doubts, worries, joys, and anxieties onto one another. For instance, the recent case of Hitachi Corporation's attempt to steal secrets from IBM is a gold mine from a psychoanalytical standpoint. It shows that whenever two organizational competitors, especially those from two very different societies, interact, they inevitably form distorted pictures of one another. Each inevitably sees the other as more evil than the other "really" is (or stronger, wiser, braver).

It would take us too far afield to describe the psychoanalytic mechanisms whereby stakeholders influence one another at this level of social analysis. We have already mentioned one such mechanism, projection. There also exist other well-studied mechanisms such as compensation, identification, and introjection. The point is that without going into these other mechanisms in depth, we have only begun to study the extreme complexity of the interactions that are possible between radically different stakeholders and the vastly different kinds of transactions in which they are capable of engaging (Wilber, 1981; Mitroff, 1983).

Human beings are complex not only because we engage in seemingly impersonal economic transactions but also because we engage in psychodynamic transactions *simultaneously*. Thus, once again, it is not so much that Figure 7 is wrong as much as it is that it is seriously incomplete. At a minimum there is potentially a *double line* of influence (economic and psychodynamic) connecting the stakeholders in Figures 7 and 8. Human beings are complex because both consciously and unconsciously we engage in transactions across very different levels of social reality simultaneously (Wilber, 1981; Mitroff, 1983).

One of the strong implications of this way of thinking is that at present we have no truly adequate theory of economics or of organizational performance. As mentioned earlier, current economic theory is largely a theory of transactions which holds only at the level of the ego, that is, conscious reality. We have no theories of *economics* or of *organizational* performance that are based on the deeper aspects of the psyche.

There is another way in which Figure 8 differs significantly from Figure 7. Some of the most recent and radical philosophical speculations concern the proposition that the world may be akin to a giant hologram (Wilber, 1982). Briefly, a hologram is a three-dimensional image which looks as if it were hovering in space. It also has an incredible property: if a part of the hologram is enlarged, the result is not merely an enlargement picture of that part; it is a fuzzy picture of the whole hologram! That is, in a hologram *the whole is contained in every part but not to the same degree of clarity*. If a hologram is a good metaphor for a complex social system, then is each stakeholder an imperfect recreation and projection of all other stakeholders? Is the performance or productivity of an organization an imperfect reflection of the performance of its stakeholders and vice versa?

The World as a Global Garden

To visualize both the power of a metaphor (for the most readable introduction to the influence of metaphors in everyday life and speech, see Lakoff and Johnson, 1980) and the image of the world it sanctions, one need turn no further than to the

Japanese. In Western society, epistemology, the branch of philosophy that is concerned with justifying what we think we know, is predominant, whereas in Japanese society, aesthetics is predominant. One cannot understand Japanese society unless one first understands that Japanese culture is infused with, above all, a deep sense of aesthetics; and, more interesting, one cannot fully appreciate the industrial structure that the Japanese have designed for their society as a whole unless one understands their particular aesthetics.

One of the deepest expressions of Japanese aesthetics is found in their concept of the garden. If one understands this conception, then certain features of their industrial system, such as the just-in-time inventory system, become more comprehensible. One also is in a better position to understand why the Japanese would orchestrate an *entire* social system to facilitate economic development. Because relationships are all important in a Japanese garden, and because no Japanese garden is or ever should be complete, one understands better why the Japanese have seen necessary to include in their industrial design institutions and relationships that proceed from specific individuals up to societal institutions such as the Ministry of International Trade and Industry that are concerned with the whole of the Japanese economy. Because this understanding is so important, we have quoted at length:

> The Japanese garden is nature on a microcosmic scale. This is not to say that it is nature imitated; rather it is nature symbolized and represented. By laying in a "grammatical" structure, the gardener develops linked patterns with concise natural forms. These in turn suggest their own essences and fill with meaning.
>
> Straight lines and perfect geometric shapes like circles and squares are rarely used except for contrast or to echo the lines of a nearby building. [That is, the Japanese garden is not nature conceived of as an orderly machine.]
>
> Asymmetrical designs and odd-numbered

groupings are favored. Not being evenly divisible, these prevent the garden from having a sense of completion and suggest the wildness of nature.

Contrast is very important. For example, a whole row of red flowers is not used, only a single red flower in a swell of green. Trees are varied in a group—flowering trees, evergreens, deciduous trees, and trees with interesting branch patterns are placed together.

The gardener suggests the passage of time by building change and motion into the garden. Trees are selected for their properties in different seasons, and fluid water-forms are contrasted with stable stones.

Much as in Japanese ink-painting, "white areas" of empty space are left in the garden for balance and to allow room for the viewer's imagination to wander.

A busy garden too full of movement or color calls undue attention to its separate parts. The gardener aims for a total effect wherein all elements are balanced to suggest quietude and repose.

Everything superfluous to the total effect of the garden is discarded. The gardener's design is complete when there is nothing more he can remove from the garden [italics ours].

There is no vista. *The garden does not have a single view but many views, each one appearing as one moves through the garden or walks around it* [italics ours]. The ideal garden is like an unrolling picture scroll that prompts surprise at every turn. But a small garden will usually have one central focus and one theme that is developed by the surrounding elements. . . .

The garden is a study in relationships. When planning, *the gardener is concerned with the interaction of every part*—slopes, colors, sounds, shapes, and movements [italics ours]. He enforces these interactions by artful placement, by using branches as frames, and by playing with perspective techniques to lengthen and bend dimensions. The shadings he adds have an almost palpable relationship and resonate through every element of the garden.

Actually, the garden's intricate and deep structure is really just a shell. For in the end, the garden speaks for itself. The length of shadows in winter, the seed pods that carpet the ground in spring, and the direction and sound of the wind are some of the many things the gardener can't control. He doesn't try to. They are as much a part of the design of his garden as the rock or lantern. By giving nature its freedom, the gardener opens himself to the new relationships that nature will suggest [Seike, Kudo, and Engel, 1980, p. 38].

One cannot aim at a good garden from the start. Indeed, even though one may begin with such an aim, there are too many elements that refuse to obey orders. Man-made objects like lanterns and water basins can be freely selected and kept under control, but stones and gravel, trees and shrubs, and even grass are quite different things. These are all splendid works of art created by nature and, like the works of art created by man, have a decided individuality. Stones, for example, are products of nature that have gone through long centuries of patient weathering. Moreover, like human beings, they have faces and hands and legs and feet. Regardless of their differences in size and type, they have facial expressions, and *every stone has a will of its own* [italics ours]. Novice gardeners are unable to read the facial expressions of stones, and gardeners with a certain degree of experience know that stones are thoroughly reluctant to obey orders, *but master gardeners know how to coax and humor these willful stones into submission* [italics

ours]. For this reason, when a master gardener
sees a stone that some heartless garden owner has
ordered to be placed in an obviously upside-down
position, he expresses his pity for it by raising its
head and lowering its feet, at the same time perhaps saying something like this: "I'm sorry for
you. You must have had a rough time of it." If another stone, at the hands of a merciless master, has
been made to face the side rather than the front,
the gardener shows sympathy for it by righting its
position, and we can imagine that he speaks to it
like this: "You really suffered, didn't you? From
now on, please face this way."

It is the same with trees and other plants. For
all their similarity, no two maple trees are ever
quite alike, nor are any two ferns. *Each plant has
its own individual shape, its own personality, its
own manner of growth* [italics ours]. When their
growth becomes disorderly, they must be trimmed
and pruned, but this does not mean that they must
be forced against their nature—their own will. The
master gardener knows this, and when the owner
of a garden comments, for example, that the recently planted bamboo seems to be of unattractive
shape, he replies, "Bamboo knows how to grow
without our telling it what to do" and leaves it
exactly as it is. In two or three years, growing according to its own will, the bamboo takes on the
graceful shape that the gardener foresaw for it
when he admonished the owner.

For such reasons as these, no matter how
much one may wish to predetermine the design of
a courtyard garden, it is next to impossible to obtain appropriate stones and trees. One may draw
the plan with extreme care, but stones and trees
have a way of not listening to what the garden
owner says. Again, no matter how many stones and
trees there might be, one is likely to discover that

not a single one of them conforms to his deepest
desires. On the other hand, quite by chance, he
may come upon a stone that he thinks would have
been a far better choice than one that is presently
in his courtyard garden. But if he discards the old
stone and replaces it with the new one and then,
like a man who has unsuccessfully taken a second
wife, discovers that he cannot live with it, it is clear
that the new stone had no affinity with the garden
after all.

It is this way with everything. Consequently, both the gardener and the garden owner must
be patient, and the courtyard garden, as though
realizing their patience, will take on a perennial
beauty that is always new and fresh. *If a man respects himself, then he must also respect the trees
and stones that nature has created. It was nature
itself, maintaining harmony among the countless
elements of its own creation, that served as the su-
preme model for the courtyard garden* [italics
ours]. Too strict an adherence to forms is equivalent, in the words of an old Japanese proverb, to
straightening the horns and killing the cow. In a
word, the formalist loses flexibility of mind and
heart, and the garden loses its life. For this reason,
a good gardener has always tried to refine and en-
rich his concepts and imaginative ideas, maintaining
a *flexible* attitude to stand him in good stead
whenever the occasion arises [italics ours] [Itoh,
1985, pp. 88-89].

No one is claiming, least of all us, that the Japanese have
explicitly or deliberately used the concept of a garden in the
design of their factories, compensation systems, and treatment
of employees, the environment, and so forth. But there is an un-
canny parallel. Most of all, given how deep aesthetics runs in
Japanese society, we would be totally surprised if there were *no*
connection.

Is it really any surprise to find a preoccupation with quality in a society that places such emphasis on the value of individual stones?

The metaphors or models of the world that have guided Western society are largely technological. Whether a simple machine, a complex system, or a hologram, these metaphors are abstract, intellectual, and technical. This is not the case with some of the other cultures with which we are in direct and intense competition. If anything, the Japanese, for example, seem to operate with an overarching metaphor of the world that combines the global garden *and* the complex system. What will it take to shift our society's predominant metaphor so that it can truly compete in a global environment?

References

Abegglen, J. C., and Stalk, G., Jr. *Kaisha: The Japanese Corporation.* New York: Basic Books, 1985.

Abernathy, W. J., and others. *Industrial Renaissance: Producing a Competitive Future for America.* New York: Basic Books, 1983.

Ackoff, R. L. *Creating the Corporate Future: Plan or Be Planned For.* New York: Wiley, 1981.

Arnold, R. "Medicine's Best Only Delayed the Inevitable." *Los Angeles Times,* Apr. 7, 1985, pp. 24, 26.

Badaracco, J. L., and Yoffie, D. B. " 'Industrial Policy': It Can't Happen Here." *Harvard Business Review,* Nov.-Dec. 1983, pp. 96-105.

Bellah, R. N., and others. *Habits of the Heart: Individualism and Commitment in American Life.* Berkeley: University of California Press, 1985.

Bernstein, P. "States Are Going Down Industrial Policy Lane." *Fortune,* Mar. 5, 1984, p. 112.

Bluestone, B., and Harrison, B. *The Deindustrialization of America.* New York: Basic Books, 1982.

Broder, J. M. "217 Safeways Will Be Equipped to Accept Bank Cards." *Los Angeles Times,* Apr. 15, 1985, p. 3.

Burck, C. G. "Will Success Spoil General Motors?" *Fortune,* Aug. 22, 1983, p. 94.

Campbell, L. B., and others. "Unlikely Partners: Company, Town, and Gown." *Harvard Business Review,* Nov.-Dec. 1985, pp. 20-28.

181

Churchman, C. W. *Thought and Wisdom*. Seaside, Calif.: Inter-systems Press, 1983.

Corwin, N. *Trivializing America*. Secaucus, N.J.: Lyle Stuart, 1983.

Davis, M. "That's Interesting." *Philosophy of Social Science,* 1971, *1*, 309–344.

Diamond, S. J. "Medicine Takes On New Look: Some Fear Aggressive Marketing Practices Will Hurt the Poor." *Los Angeles Times,* Feb. 10, 1985, pp. 1, 5.

Dobrzynski, J., and others. "Fighting Back: It Can Work, Some Companies Are Finding Ways to Keep Japan from Always Winning." *Business Week,* Aug. 26, 1985, p. 62.

Dolan, M. "Poor Management for Shuttle Charged." *Los Angeles Times,* June 4, 1986, p. 1.

Engardio, P. "Textile Imports Are Swamping Even the Best Companies: No Matter How Fast the Industry Reforms, Hundreds More Mills Will Go Under." *Business Week,* Sept. 16, 1985, p. 50.

Fallows, J. "America's Changing Economic Landscape." *The Atlantic,* Mar. 1985a, p. 56.

Fallows, J. "The Three Fiscal Crises." *Atlantic Monthly,* Sept. 1985b, pp. 19–20.

Fisher, A. B. "Behind the Hype at GM's Saturn." *Fortune,* 1985, *112* (11), 34–49.

Gannes, S. "Back-to-Basics Computers with Sports-Car Speed." *Fortune,* Sept. 30, 1985, p. 98.

Gevirtz, D. *Business Plan for America: An Entrepreneur's Manifesto*. New York: Putnam, 1984.

Gibson, R. "Firms Warming to Joint Ventures Abroad: Despite Culture Clashes, U.S. Multinationals Find Partners Can Be Assets." *Los Angeles Times,* June 9, 1985, p. 5.

Ginzberg, E., and Vojta, G. *Beyond Human Scale: The Large Corporation at Risk*. New York: Basic Books, 1985.

Greenwald, J., Witteman, P., and Ungehauer, F. " 'Lulu Is Home Now': GM Buys Hughes and Heads for the 21st Century." *Time,* Jun. 17, 1985, p. 57.

Greenwald, J., and others. "Pressure from Abroad." *Time,* Apr. 8, 1985, pp. 52–53.

Hawken, P., Ogilvy, J., and Schwartz, P. *Seven Tomorrows: Toward a Voluntary History.* New York: Bantam Books, 1982.

Hiltzik, M. "Banks Enter New World of High Risk: Huge Commitments Are Hidden from Their Balance Sheets." *Los Angeles Times,* Oct. 27, 1985, pp. 1, 5.

Hoerr, J. "Now Unions Are Helping to Run the Business." *Business Week,* Dec. 24, 1984, p. 69.

Itoh, T. *Space and Illusion in the Japanese Garden.* Tokyo: Weatherhill/Tankosha, 1985.

Jameson, S., and Redburn, T. "Inside MITI: How Key Japanese Unit Forges Industrial Consensus." *Los Angeles Times,* May 23, 1983, p. 3.

Jonas, N. "A Strategy for Revitalizing Industry." *Business Week,* Mar. 3, 1986, pp. 84-85.

Jones, N., and others. "How the Tax Code Is Feeding Merger Mania." *Business Week,* May 27, 1985, pp. 62-64.

Kantrow, A. M. (ed.). "The Political Realities of Industrial Policy." *Harvard Business Review,* Sept.-Oct. 1983, pp. 76-86.

Keppel, B. "Humana Will Test Computer That Could Cut Hospital Labor Expenses." *Los Angeles Times,* Sept. 8, 1985, p. 4.

Kilmann, R. H. *Beyond the Quick Fix: Managing Five Tracks to Organizational Success.* San Francisco: Jossey-Bass, 1984.

Kilmann, R. H., Saxton, M. J., Serpa, R., and Associates (eds.). *Gaining Control of the Corporate Culture.* San Francisco: Jossey-Bass, 1985.

Kissinger, H. A. *Nuclear Weapons and Foreign Policy.* New York: Norton, 1969.

Kissinger, H. A. "U.S. Frictions, Japan Factions: Persuading in Trading Means Knowing a Partner." *Los Angeles Times,* Oct. 6, 1984, p. 2.

Kraft, S. "Hospitals for Profit: What Price Care?" *Los Angeles Times,* Mar. 31, 1985, pp. 1, 34-35.

Kramer, O. S. "Putting More Pain into Bank Failures." *Fortune,* Feb. 20, 1984, pp. 135-142.

Lakoff, G., and Johnson, M. *Metaphors We Live By.* Chicago: University of Chicago Press, 1980.

Lawler, E. E. III. *High-Involvement Management.* San Francisco: Jossey-Bass, 1986.

Lawrence, P. R., and Dyer, D. *Renewing American Industry.* New York: Free Press, 1983.

Linstone, H. *The Multiperspective Method.* Reading, Mass.: Addison-Wesley, 1984.

Louis, A. M. "America's New Economy: How to Manage in It." *Fortune,* Jun. 23, 1986.

McComas, M. "More Capital Won't Cure What Ails Banks." *Fortune,* Jan. 7, 1985, pp. 80–86.

Magaziner, I. C., and Reich, R. B. *Minding America's Business: The Decline and Rise of the American Economy.* New York: Vintage Books, 1983.

Magnet, M. "How Top Managers Make a Company's Toughest Decision." *Fortune,* 1985, p. 56.

Maruyama, M. "Alternative Concepts of Management: Insights from Asia and Africa." *Asia Pacific Journal of Management,* 1984, *1* (Jan.), pp. 100–110.

Maruyama, M. "Mindscapes: How to Understand Specific Situations in Multicultural Management." *Asia Pacific Journal of Management,* 1985, *2* (May), 125–149.

Mason, R. O., and Mitroff, I. I. *Challenging Strategic Planning Assumptions.* New York: Wiley, 1981.

Mill, J. S. *A System of Logic.* New York: Longmans, Green, 1872.

Mills, D. Q., and Lovell, M. R., Jr. "Enhancing Competitiveness: The Contribution of Employee Relations." In B. R. Scott and G. C. Lodge (eds.), *U.S. Competitiveness in the World Economy.* Boston: Harvard Business School Press, 1985, pp. 455–478.

Mitroff, I. I. *The Subjective Side of Science.* Amsterdam: Elsevier, 1974.

Mitroff, I. I. *Stakeholders of the Organizational Mind: Toward a New View of Organizational Policy Making.* San Francisco: Jossey-Bass, 1983.

Mitroff, I. I. "The Complete and Utter Failure of Traditional Thinking in Comprehending the Nuclear Dilemma: Why It's Impossible to Formulate a Paradox-Free Theory of Nuclear

Strategy." *Journal of Technological Forecasting and Social Change,* 1986, *29,* 51–72.

Mitroff, I. I., and Kilmann, R. H. *Methodological Approaches to Social Science.* San Francisco: Jossey-Bass, 1978.

Mitroff, I. I., and Kilmann, R. H. *Corporate Tragedies: Product Tampering, Sabotage, and Other Catastrophes.* New York: Praeger, 1984.

Mitroff, I. I., Mason, R. O., and Barabba, V. P. *The 1980 Census: Policy Making amid Turbulence.* Lexington, Mass.: Lexington Books, 1983.

Moreland, P. "The Old Ways Are Fading: Other Options Force Doctors to Compete." *Los Angeles Times,* Feb. 10, 1985, pp. 1, 10.

Morris, C. R. "Ohio Offers a Lesson in Banking: There Are No Safe Havens." *Los Angeles Times,* Mar. 31, 1985, p. 3.

Navaro, P. *The Policy Game: How Special Interests and Ideologues Are Stealing America.* New York: Wiley, 1984.

Nelson, H. "Luck—and Money—Help Preemie Beat Odds." *Los Angeles Times,* Apr. 7, 1985, p. 24.

Nelson, H., and Roark, A. C. "Health Care Crisis: Less for More." *Los Angeles Times,* Apr. 7, 1985, pp. 1, 24–28.

Osborne, D. "Business in Space." *Atlantic Monthly,* May 1985, p. 51.

O'Toole, J. "Declining Innovation: The Failure of Success. A Summary Report of the Seventh Twenty Year Forecast Project." Center for Futures Research, Graduate School of Business, University of Southern California, 1983, pp. 1–28.

Peterson, J. "HMOs Scramble for Health-Care Funds of Elderly: Alternative to Medicare Offers Savings, but Causes Confusion." *Los Angeles Times,* Jun. 16, 1985, pp. 1, 6.

Phillips, K. *Staying on Top: The Business Case for a National Industrial Strategy.* New York: Random House, 1984.

Piore, M. J., and Sabel, C. F. *The Second Industrial Divide.* New York: Basic Books, 1984.

Postman, N. *Amusing Ourselves to Death: Public Discourse in the Age of Show Business.* New York: Viking Penguin, 1985.

Reich, R. B. *The Next American Frontier.* New York: Times Books, 1983.

Reich, R. B. "Toward a New Public Philosophy." *Atlantic Monthly*, May 1985, pp. 68-79.

Risen, J. "GM's Tuscaloosa Plant Turns Into University Lab." *Los Angeles Times*, Oct. 6, 1985, pp. 1, 5.

Schein, E. H. *Organizational Culture and Leadership: A Dynamic View*. San Francisco: Jossey-Bass, 1985.

Schumacher. E. F. *Small Is Beautiful: Economics as if People Mattered*. New York: Harper & Row, 1973.

Scott, B. R., and Lodge, G. C. (eds.). *U.S. Competitiveness in the World Economy*. Boston: Harvard Business School Press, 1985.

Seike, K., Kudo, M., and Engel, D. H. *A Japanese Touch for Your Garden*. Tokyo: Kodansha International, 1980.

Sethi, S. P., Nobuaki, and Swanson, C. L. *The False Promise of the Japanese Miracle*. Boston: Pitman, 1984.

Sheets, K. R. "U.S. Minimills Getting Caught in Steel Trap: Too Much of a Good Thing—Small Steelmakers Are the Latest to Learn that Success Can Be Its Own Worst Enemy." *U.S. News and World Report*, Dec. 9, 1985, p. 51.

Shiver, J. "Doctors Seek Advice on Starting a Healthy Practice." *Los Angeles Times*, Feb. 10, 1985, pp. 1, 8.

"Showdown in Detroit: The Future of the Industry—and the UAW—Is at Stake in the Auto Talks." *Business Week*, Sept. 10, 1984, pp. 104-105.

Smith, R. J. "Crisis Management Under Strain." *Science*, 1984, *225* (Aug. 31), 908.

Smith, R. J. "Inquiry Faults Shuttle Management." *Science*, 1986, *232*, 1488-1489.

Starr, P. *The Social Transformation of American Medicine: The Rise of a Sovereign Profession and the Making of a Vast Industry*. New York: Basic Books, 1982.

Stokes, H. S. "Lost Samurai: The Withered Soul of Postwar Japan." *Harpers Magazine*, Oct. 1985, pp. 55-63.

"Swapping Work Rules for Jobs at G.E.'s 'Factory of the Future.' " *Business Week*, Sept. 10, 1984, pp. 43-46.

"The World Can't Shrug off a U.S. Showdown for Long." *Business Week*, Dec. 10, 1984, p. 51.

Thurow, L. *The Zero-Sum Solution: Building a World-Class American Economy*. New York: Simon & Schuster, 1985a.

Thurow, L. "A Time to Dismantle the World Economy." *The Economist,* Nov. 9, 1985b, pp. 21–26.

Tocqueville, A. de. *Democracy in America.* Vols. I and II. New York: Vintage Books, 1945. (Originally published 1835, 1840.)

Toffler, A. *The Third Wave.* New York: William Morrow, 1980.

Treadwell, D. "South Carolina Mill Town Weaves a New Economy." *Los Angeles Times,* Oct. 27, 1985, p. 13.

Tuchman, B. W. *The March of Folly: From Troy to Vietnam.* New York: Knopf, 1984.

Vogel, E. F. *Comeback. Case by Case: Building the Resurgence of American Business.* New York: Simon & Schuster, 1985.

Whitefield, D. "Entrepreneurs Wanted. Big Firms' New Motto: Think Small." *Los Angeles Times,* Nov. 27, 1985, p. 1.

Whiteside, D., and others. "How GM's Saturn Could Run Rings Around Old-Style Carmakers." *Business Week,* Jan. 28, 1985, p. 128.

Wilber, K. *Up from Eden.* New York: Doubleday, 1981.

Wilber, K. (ed.). *The Holographic Paradigm.* London: Shambhala, 1982.

"Will Money Managers Wreck the Economy? Their Short-Term View Derails Companies' Long-Term Plans." *Business Week,* Aug. 13, 1984, pp. 88–94.

Woutat, D. "Rust Bowl a Magnet for Investments." *Los Angeles Times,* Nov. 19, 1984, p. 20.

Yates, B. *The Decline and Fall of the American Automobile Industry.* New York: Vintage Books, 1984.

Index